WHAT GOD WANTS EVERY DAD *to* KNOW

JAMES MERRITT

HARVEST HOUSE PUBLISHERS
EUGENE, OREGON

Cover design by Koechel Peterson & Associates, Inc., Minneapolis, Minnesota

Cover photo © altrendo images / Stockbyte / Thinkstock

Published in association with the literary agency of Wolgemuth & Associates, Inc.

WHAT GOD WANTS EVERY DAD TO KNOW
Copyright © 2013 by James Merritt
Published by Harvest House Publishers
Eugene, Oregon 97402
www.harvesthousepublishers.com

Library of Congress Cataloging-in-Publication Data
    Merritt, James Gregory, 1952-
    What God wants every dad to know / James Merritt.
        pages cm
    ISBN 978-0-7369-5008-4 (pbk.)
    ISBN 978-0-7369-5009-1 (eBook)
    1. Fatherhood—Religious aspects—Christianity. 2. Fathers—Religious life. 3. Parent and child—Religious aspects—Christianity. I. Title.
    BV4529.17.M47 2013
    248.8'421--dc23

                                                                2012044856

Printed in the United States of America

17 18 19 20 21 22 / BP-JH / 10 9 8 7 6 5 4 3

"Buy this book for every father you know! It takes the time-tested truths of Proverbs and applies them to the task of fathering in a way that is both helpful and hopeful."

—**Rick Warren**, pastor, Saddleback Valley Community Church, author of *The Purpose Driven Life*

"Leadership is my heart and passion. The one thing a leader cannot delegate is his family. Using Proverbs as his source, James Merritt has written an outstanding book that will empower every father to lead his children to godly success. It is both powerful in its content and practical in its application. Dad, if you want to read a book that will change you and your family, read this one."

—**John C. Maxwell**, leadership expert, author, and speaker

"Paying heed to the best of wisdom, and understanding the worst threats, James Merritt gives answers that can transform the heart of a dad. In a time of broken relationships, here is a book that builds bridges on strong foundations. The joy of committed fatherhood has an unparalleled reward. James Merritt helps us navigate through the perils to win this grand prize of godly children."

—**Ravi Zacharias**, president, Ravi Zacharias International Ministries

"With the wisdom of a PhD, the warning of a pastor, the wit of a communicator, and the warmth of a father, James Merritt has written a contemporary classic on the one subject we must not fail—fatherhood. This is must reading for busy men who understand that it profits a man nothing to gain the whole world and lose his children. I use this book for my devotions. Having grown up in six broken homes, this book serves to motivate, model, and mentor me in my life quest—being an effective father. I am eternally grateful. I need such a mentor."

—**Jay Strack**, president and founder, Student Leadership University

"James Merritt is my friend and counselor. Most of all he is a father... His message about child rearing is as simple and straightforward as the Sermon on the Mount or the Golden Rule. He is exactly the right messenger."

—**Honorable John Linder**, former US Congressman from Georgia

I dedicate this book to my three sons,
James, Jonathan, and Joshua.
No dad could love you more or be prouder of you.

CONTENTS

Being Fathers in a World of Fatherlessness

"Nothing I've ever done has given me more joys and rewards than being a father to my children."

BILL COSBY, ACTOR

My knees nearly buckled when the door swung open and the nurse motioned for me. "Mr. Merritt, you may come in now," she said. I had been pacing back and forth outside the hospital delivery room, but now my legs moved in one direction. Through one door and then two, I approached my exhausted wife lying behind a makeshift curtain.

And that's when I heard it for the first time. A cry from the most beautiful baby—from *my* baby. My wife fought back tears as she looked at me and proclaimed, "We have a baby boy!" Lips quivering and hands shaking, I whispered back to her, "I'm a dad!"

You'd need to be a parent yourself to know the emotions flooding me the moment I laid eyes on my firstborn son. Elation. Pride. Apprehension. But perhaps greater than all these sensations was the deep sense of responsibility I felt for the future of this child. I knew I had just been assigned one of the greatest tasks a man will ever face: being a dad.

My mind raced with the many things I wanted for my new

son, James Jr. I desired for him to be healthy and happy and to decide to follow Jesus when he was old enough to understand what that meant. I wanted him to grow strong on the outside and tough on the inside, prepared for the harsh realities of the modern world.

"God give my son the spiritual and moral weaponry needed to *win*, not just survive, the battle called life," I would pray in the coming months. "As he grows into a man, help him to do more than make a living. Empower him to make a life for himself that would honor You."

Sadly, too few parents today take their roles so seriously. Louis Sullivan, former secretary of Health and Human Services, delivered a speech to the Institute of American Values in the early 1990s and made this startling observation: "Though our society is only beginning to recognize it, the greatest family challenge of our era is fatherlessness...The adverse consequences of a father's absence cannot be reduced to only a decline in income. It is one thing to substitute for a missing father's paycheck. His attention, his guidance, his discipline, and his love, however, are not easily replaced."

Sullivan's words are as true today as when he spoke them. Absentee fatherhood is becoming increasingly recognized as a strong contributor to the cultural, moral, and spiritual meltdown of our nation. Children growing up without fathers may be the number one social problem facing America today. But absenteeism is not confined to the inner city, nor caused solely by out-of-wedlock fathering. It is a phenomenon that is affecting homes in every community, with divorce and workaholism as two primary culprits.[1]

> The most endangered species in America is
> not the spotted owl nor the snail darter,
> but the responsible father.

We live in a generation that, for the first time in American history, has failed to understand this. The most endangered species in America is not the spotted owl nor the snail darter, but the responsible father. More children will go to sleep tonight in a fatherless home than ever before in our nation's history. Consider the following:

- In 1960, fewer than six million children lived in single parent families. Today, the number is 22 million—27 percent of children under the age of 21.

- 43 percent of American children live in a home in which their biological father is absent.

- Before they reach the age of eighteen, more than half of our nation's children are likely to spend at least a significant portion of their childhoods living apart from their fathers.

- For the first time in American history, the average child will live for a significant period of time without a father at home.[2]

Just how serious is this problem of fatherlessness? This statement drives it home with irresistible force: "Fatherlessness is the most harmful demographic trend of this generation. It is the leading cause of declining child well-being in our society. *It is also the engine driving our most urgent social problems,* from crime to adolescent pregnancy to child sexual abuse to domestic violence against women."[3]

Have a hard time believing this? Then consider that according to a study published in *The Journal of Research and Crime and Delinquency,* the best indicator of violent crime in a community is not race, income, or employment, but *the proportion of fatherless families.*[4]

The devastation fatherlessness leaves in its wake is staggering. Think about the *emotional* devastation of fatherlessness:

- Fatherless children are anywhere from 100 to 200 percent more likely to have emotional and behavioral problems.

- A child who comes from a fatherless home is 68 percent more likely to use drugs or alcohol, far more likely to become sexually active at an early age, and three times as likely to commit a violent crime.[5]

- 63 percent of teenagers who attempt suicide live in fatherless homes.

- Most runaways leave homes that are fatherless.

- Fatherless sons are 300 percent more likely to become incarcerated in state juvenile institutions. Seventy percent of juveniles in long-term correctional facilities grew up without a father in the home.

- Fatherless daughters are 53 percent more likely to marry as teenagers, 111 percent more likely to have children as teenagers, 164 percent more likely to have an out-of-wedlock birth.

- Fatherless daughters who marry have a 92 percent higher divorce rate, and fatherless sons are 35 percent more likely to experience marital failure.[6]

- Eighty percent of teenagers admitted to psychiatric hospitals come from fatherless homes.[7]

Then there is the *intellectual* devastation. Children who come from fatherless homes:

- Display more antisocial behavior.

- Are 50 percent more likely to have learning disabilities.

- Do worse in school and are three times as likely to drop out as children who grow up in a home with a father.[8]

- Only 11.6 percent of children living with both parents repeat a grade in school. But for children of never married mothers, the number is 29.7 percent; and for children living with a divorced mother, it is 21.5 percent.[9]

Finally there is the *physical* devastation. Children who come from broken families where the father is absent are twenty to forty times more likely to suffer health problems than children who live with both parents.

> We are experiencing an epidemic of physically absent fathers, but we also have a crisis of emotionally and spiritually absent fathers in America.

Though these numbers speak to an epidemic of physically absent fathers—one that has only worsened in recent years—we also have a crisis of emotionally and spiritually absent fathers in America. Dads need to rediscover the important job they've been given. We need to partner with our wives in the nitty-gritty business of building character in our children. We need to showcase a life well lived for them, and help them avoid unnecessary mistakes that can shipwreck them. Few things are as important as this task.

In my office hangs a picture of me, James Jr., my middle son, Jonathan, and President George H.W. Bush. We had been invited by a friend to meet the president at a dinner in Atlanta, and I'll always remember how gracious he was to my sons, speaking to them as if they were his own grandchildren. The picture is a relic from my daddy days and looking on it never fails to trigger a smile.

But that picture also reminds me of the answer President Bush gave when asked about his greatest accomplishment in life. He could have recounted his experience as a fighter pilot in World War II and how he was shot down and had to ditch his plane in the sea. Or his public service as ambassador to China, as vice president, and then as president of the U.S. Or that he was the commander in chief who led us to victory in the Persian Gulf War with few casualties. Or that he had two sons serve as state governors with one becoming commander in chief himself. Yet Bush said with both pride and finality, "My children still come home." As a father of three grown sons with careers of their own, I can attest to the truth in the forty-first president's words.

Your children's destiny depends, in part, on your presence in their life. Not on the level of their education or their natural talents or even their charisma—it depends on *you*.

Visionizing the Father You Want to Be

Kruger National Park is the largest wildlife preserve in South Africa. Thirty years ago the elephant population exceeded the park's capacity to sustain it, and a decision was made to kill off some of the adults and relocate some of the younger elephants. These young bulls were resettled in Pilanesberg National Park.

All seemed well for a few years. Then an unexplained slaughter of rhinos began taking place in Pilanesberg. It appeared to be an open and shut case of poachers until surveillance was set up. Shockingly the culprits were the young hyperaggressive bull elephants who were harassing the rhinos, chasing them relentlessly and goring them to death with their tusks.

This puzzled the experts as elephants generally are docile, reserved, and rarely attack other animals without provocation.

Why were these young elephants becoming roving thugs? It turned out that these "orphans" had developed into a gang replete with gang leaders. Without older bull elephants functioning as authoritative, stabilizing role models, the younger elephants reverted to much more primitive behavior.

What was the solution? Older, more mature bulls were brought to Pilanesberg as a "foster father/big brother" experiment. Within weeks, discipline was restored as the younger elephants began to bond with and follow the older elephants, imitating them and exhibiting more acceptable behavior. There were no reports of any other killed rhinos. Even in the animal world the presence of father figures is essential to civil behavior, discipline, and relational decorum with others.[10]

Dad, think of life as a series of snapshots that culminate in the big picture or as a series of tests that lead to the final exam. In his best-selling book *The Seven Habits of Highly Effective People,* Stephen Covey identifies one of the seven habits as "Begin with the End in Mind."[11] As we begin this journey into a fresh look at fatherhood from a uniquely biblical perspective, I want you to begin to visualize—no, make that "visionize"—the man you want your boy or the woman you want your daughter to become.

Will you be an absent, docile father? Or will you be a loving, disciplining presence in your child's life? Your choice will be felt for generations.

It is every father's role, right, and responsibility for each of their children to help the child to sit down and the adult to stand up. But more than this, to help them stand in a way that they, in turn, can help their children stand as well. As Dwight L. Moody said, "If you want to know what kind of father you were, don't look at your children; look at your grandchildren." Your children are just a generational link in a chain that will reach far beyond your lifetime. Now that I have two grandchildren—my best buddy, Harper, and my precious princess, Presley—I must tell you I am laser-focused on their development. I want my son to be a true father to his children, the kind that will pass down to them the baton of a love for God, family, and friends.

The Window Closes Quickly

Take it from someone who has seen the blur of infancy turn into the flash of adolescence and morph into adulthood: The window of opportunity you have with your kids is not open wide. It closes at supersonic speed. Your kids want your time and as much of it as they can get.

> The window of opportunity you have with your kids is not open wide. It closes at supersonic speed.

When Jonathan was still in elementary school, I took an opportunity to form one of the sweetest memories of my life. I showed up in the middle of the day, out of the blue, and checked him out of class. When he was called to the office, he was shocked to see me, thinking something was wrong. That little third-grader's eyes lit up when I told him I had a surprise adventure to take him on. We were going to Stone Mountain Park, a place that he loved not far from our home. I can still see that angelic smile on his face as the double joy of getting out of school *and* going to one of his favorite places totally made his day.

We spent the entire day together, riding the train around the mountain and a horse-drawn carriage through the park. We ate funnel cakes and belly-laughed together. As I write these words, I do so with tears, wishing I had far more of those memories. But I'll never forget the way he looked at me that day. He wasn't wearing my cape and he didn't have my logo on his chest. But for a brief moment, I knew I had been the kind of father he needed me to be. Looking back over my life, I wish I'd created more of those kinds of moments. Few things are more valuable for either person than when a man becomes the father his child needs him to be.

Perhaps you are beginning your journey as a dad or maybe you're knee-deep in the pond of parenting. Either way, you recognize the importance of the task you've been given, and you're filled with the same desires that flooded my soul in that delivery room more than three decades ago. Take it from me, the fatherhood years fly by at warp speed. In the blink of an eye your children will go from calling you Da-da to Daddy to Dad. And in another blink, you'll wish they'd call you at all. The window of opportunity to get it right shrinks rapidly, and every day counts to help the boy or girl to sit down and the man or woman to stand up. Perhaps the most frustrating thing about being a parent is that just about the time you figure it out, you're out of a job!

I've come to realize that the first task of fathering is accepting you won't do it perfectly. You'll speak words that you'll regret and take actions that will grieve you later. No matter how much you do for and with your kids, you'll wish you had done more. I traveled the world with my three sons, attended all their sports and school events, coached some of their teams, led them in family devotions around the breakfast table, memorized Scripture with them, took them on mission trips, and made sure to guard our precious weekly family nights. Yet I wish I had spent more time pouring into their lives.

In the pages that follow, you'll encounter the lessons I've learned—often the hard way—and the wisdom I've accumulated over my years as a dad. But more importantly, you'll touch and taste the surprising advice God has for you and your child. When my sweaty palms first cradled my son in that delivery room and

I held him up to the light, my spirit burned with a desire to help him grow into a man after God's own heart. I have a hunch that same desire now ignites you too. My prayer is that you're about to discover divine wisdom that will spark the fire of your resolve and give you confidence in the great task you've been given.

1

God's Letter to Dads

*"Fathers and mothers have lost the idea that the
highest aspiration they might have for their children
is for them to be wise…Specialized competence
and success are all that they can imagine."*

ALLAN BLOOM, *THE CLOSING OF THE AMERICAN MIND*

Shortly after my first child was born, I began scouring book-
stores and libraries for parenting books. I wanted to be a
good dad—no, a great one—and I knew I needed some
help. I began wading through stacks of books by psychiatrists,
psychologists, pediatricians, and preachers searching for the best
parenting advice I could find.

If you did this after your first child was born, you know it can
become an exercise in frustration. Everyone seems to have an
opinion on how to successfully raise children and they often dif-
fer substantially. I soon found myself drowning in expert advice
without any way to determine which opinions to incorporate and
which to toss out. Meanwhile, my child was growing older, learning to walk and to speak broken English. Time was running out.

One day, I found myself reading a different kind of book. An
ancient one called Proverbs. It was written, not by a counselor, but
by a king. And in it I found exactly what i had been looking for.

Sometime before King Solomon wrote this book, God gave

him the opportunity of a lifetime. He did something for Solomon that, as far as the Bible reveals, He had never done before and never did again. He asked Solomon the most amazing question an omnipotent, infinite God can ask a weak, finite human: "That night God appeared to Solomon and said to him, 'Ask for whatever you want me to give you.'"[1]

Let that sink in for a moment. The Creator God said to a created man, "Your wish is my command." Solomon was given carte blanche by the One in whose dictionary the word *impossible* does not exist.

For King Solomon this was not just about hitting the divine lottery; this was a test. At the tender age of twenty, he was about to find out who he was in the deepest core of his soul. An anonymous thinker wrote these words:

> Tell me your dreams, and I will read the riddle of your life. Tell me your prayers, and I will write the history of your soul. Tell me your askings, and I will tell you your gettings. Tell me what you seek, and I will tell you what you are…I do not wish to know your possessions…only your wants. I do not care to know what you have, only what you have not and desire to have; not your attainments, but what you have not yet attained and follow after; that which comes to you in your victories by day and your dreams by night, the ideal you set before you, the things you approve as excellent, what you seek after and have given your heart to, these are the measure of a man.[2]

An egotistical person would have asked for fame. A materialistic person would have asked for wealth. An ambitious person would have asked for power. I dare say only one out of a billion people would have asked for something outside of one of those three categories—but not Solomon. How does Solomon fill in the blank? "Give me wisdom and knowledge, that I may lead this people, for who is able to govern this great people of yours?" he says.[3]

It was the very thing I was looking for. And God granted Solomon's wish by giving him something more valuable than wealth, more satisfying than fame, and more exhilarating than power. Indeed, all these other things became a byproduct of the gift of wisdom.

God went on to make a promise to Solomon:

> God said to Solomon, "Since this is your heart's desire and you have not asked for wealth, possessions or honor, nor for the death of your enemies, and since you have not asked for a long life but for wisdom and knowledge to govern my people over whom I have made you king, therefore wisdom and knowledge will be given you. And I will also give you wealth, possessions and honor, such as no king who was before you ever had and none after you will have."[4]

Did God keep His word? Well, consider this. What would you have if you crossed an Arab sheik, the president of the United States, Socrates, and Mickey Mouse? You would have the richest, most powerful, wisest, and most famous person in the world—an apt description of King Solomon in his day.

- Solomon became the chief executive officer of the world's greatest empire.
- By his trading skills, he was acclaimed as the world's foremost merchant.
- As the leading shipping magnate, he had a fleet of merchant ships that sailed throughout the world, collecting treasures.
- By his wealth he easily topped the Forbes 400 list.

- He was a master builder who constructed mammoth projects.

- His architectural designs became the world's most important buildings.

- He built vineyards, gardens, parks, and reservoirs.

- Tired of commerce, he turned to science, relentlessly pursuing the classification of nature.

- He was his own chairman of the Joint Chiefs of Staff, building a vast army to defend and conquer.

- He became the poet laureate of his nation.

- He had a distinguished career as a writer.

- He was a singularly gifted musician.[5]

Solomon learned the incredible worth of wisdom, enjoyed her benefits, and so wrote, "Wisdom is more precious than rubies, and nothing you desire can compare with her."[6]

God's Treasure Chest

This background brings us to the book of Proverbs. Proverbs is a treasure chest containing the nuggets of wisdom that Solomon mined from the heart of God. When you study Proverbs, you strike the mother lode of heavenly wisdom for earthly living.

But dad, *Proverbs is far more than that.*

One of the great habits any dad can adopt is to read one chapter in Proverbs every day. Why? Because you need and should want wisdom—not the counterfeit, pseudo-intellectual knowledge this world manufactures, but wisdom poured straight out of the bucket of God's heart.

For years I came to this river of wisdom, panning each day for some golden nugget of heavenly brilliance that I could stash away in my pouch. I never gave much thought either to the One who had buried these nuggets within Holy Scripture or why He even bothered. Then I made an amazing discovery:

As I was reading Proverbs one morning, two words suddenly leaped off the page. I had never noticed them before. The words were, *my son.* I hurriedly ran to my computer and pulled up the phrase on my concordance.

> Listen, *my son,* to your father's instruction
>   and do not forsake your mother's teaching
>   (Proverbs 1:8).
>
> *My son,* if sinful men entice you,
>   do not give in to them (1:10).
>
> *My son,* do not go along with them,
>   do not set foot on their paths (1:15).
>
> *My son,* do not forget my teaching,
>   but keep my commands in your heart (3:1).
>
> *My son,* do not despise the LORD's discipline,
>   and do not resent his rebuke (3:11).
>
> *My son,* do not let wisdom and understanding out of
>   your sight,
>   preserve sound judgment and discretion (3:21).
>
> Listen, *my son,* and accept what I say,
>   and the years of your life will be many (4:10).
>
> *My son,* pay attention to my wisdom,
>   turn your ear to my words of insight (5:1).
>
> Why, *my son,* be intoxicated with another man's wife?
>   Why embrace the bosom of a wayward woman?
>   (5:20).
>
> *My son,* if you have put up security for your neighbor,
>   if you have shaken hands in pledge for a stranger,
> you have been trapped by what you said,
>   ensnared by the words of your mouth.

So do this, *my son,* to free yourself,
　　since you have fallen into your neighbor's hands:
Go—to the point of exhaustion—
　　and give your neighbor no rest! (6:1-3).

My son, keep your father's command
　　and do not forsake your mother's teaching (6:20).

My son, keep my words
　　and store up my commands within you (7:1).

Stop listening to instruction, *my son,*
　　and you will stray from the words of knowledge
　　　　(19:27).

My son, if your heart is wise,
　　then my heart will be glad indeed (23:15).

Listen, *my son,* and be wise,
　　and set your heart on the right path (23:19).

My son, give me your heart
　　and let your eyes delight in my ways (23:26).

Eat honey, *my son,* for it is good;
　　honey from the comb is sweet to your taste (24:13).

Fear the Lord and the king, *my son,*
　　and do not join with rebellious officials (24:21).

Be wise, *my son,* and bring joy to my heart;
　　then I can answer anyone who treats me with
　　　　contempt (27:11).

Listen, *my son*! Listen, son of my womb!
　　Listen, *my son,* the answer to my prayers! (31:2).

> Proverbs is not just a book;
> it is a letter from a father to his child.

Twenty-three times this phrase is used. In addition, "my sons" or "my children" is used four times (Proverbs 4:1; 5:7; 7:24; 8:32). As I meditated on this startling discovery, suddenly the lights came on. Proverbs is not just a book; it is a letter from a father to his child.

Solomon did not sit down one day in the portico of his palace and, out of sheer boredom and with nothing else to do, say, "I think I'll write a book on wisdom and show how sharp I really am." Rather, I believe he came to realize that his greatest legacy was not his money, his fame, or his power, but his family. He was passing on what God—the giver of all wisdom—wants every dad to know.

Indeed, the theme of the book is captured in something Solomon's father, David, said to him many years before:

The beginning of wisdom is this: Get wisdom.
Though it cost all you have, get understanding.[7]

In short, Proverbs is more than a random collection of pithy maxims strung together willy-nilly; *it is godly wisdom passed down from a father to his children to enable them to maximize their potential for living a God-blessed, meaningful life.* In other words, Proverbs is a tool that a dad can use to help his children "wise up in a dumbing down world." When I saw this, I began to hear the heart of a father pulsate on every page.

> Proverbs is a letter *from* a father *about* fathers and *to* fathers. It not only teaches a father how to *lead* his children, but how to *live* before his children.

Then my eyes were opened to still another unique twist to this "letter." This letter to a son is *from a father.* The book begins with this salutation: "Listen, my son, to your *father's* instruction" (1:8).[8]

The word *father* is used eighteen times in Proverbs.[9] I believe this is another key that unlocks the meaning of this book. Proverbs is a letter *from* a father *about* fathers and *to* fathers. It not only teaches a father how to *lead* his children, but how to *live* before his children.

Living Beyond Your Lifetime

Dad, stop right here and nail this next statement to the door of your heart. *Wisdom is the one gift you can pass on to your children that will last beyond your lifetime.* You can leave your children money, but eventually they will spend it. You can leave your children property, but eventually they will sell it. You can leave your family trinkets and toys, but eventually they will either lose them or give them away. But when you leave them wisdom, your gift lasts forever!

Proverbs 4 is a revealing picture both of a precious memory in Solomon's mind and the purpose for Proverbs that was in Solomon's heart. First, he recalled his days as a young child when he was the apple of David's eye. Take in the picture he painted for us:

> Listen, my sons, to a father's instruction;
> > pay attention and gain understanding.
> I give you sound learning,
> > so do not forsake my teaching.
> For I too was a son to my father,
> > still tender, and cherished by my mother.
> Then he taught me, and he said to me,
> > "Take hold of my words with all your heart;
> > keep my commands, and you will live."[10]

David was not only a king in a castle; he was a professor in his home. This passage reveals the centerpiece of the advice David

gave to young Solomon. He drilled one thought into the heart
and mind of Solomon early on:

> Get wisdom, get understanding;
>> do not forget my words or turn away from them.
> Do not forsake wisdom, and she will protect you;
>> love her, and she will watch over you.
> The beginning of wisdom is this: Get wisdom.
>> Though it cost all you have, get understanding.[11]

This was what happened to Solomon in the past, as a son.
But Solomon wrote Proverbs in the present, as a father. He had
moved from the role of student to teacher. So he said,

> Listen, my son, accept what I say,
>> and the years of your life will be many.
> I instruct you in the way of wisdom
>> and lead you along straight paths.[12]

Solomon took the wisdom baton from his father and wanted
to pass it on to his children. What Solomon did, you can do, for
you have the manual of wisdom in Proverbs. You can take the
baton of wisdom from the heavenly Father and pass it down to
your own children.

> We live in a world that is drowning in knowledge
> yet starving for wisdom.

God placed Solomon's wisdom in His Word, which tells us that
this was not human wisdom raised to a supernatural height, but
supernatural wisdom lowered to human understanding. From the
beginning, Solomon repeatedly encouraged fathers to dive into
this ocean of wisdom and drink from its fountain of truth. Lest

you think the water is too deep and wisdom is beyond you, listen first to what the wisest man in the world told us about wisdom.

Wisdom: If You Seek It, You Shall Find It

We live in a world that is drowning in knowledge yet starving for wisdom. It was a wise eye that made this salient observation:

> Since 1955 knowledge has doubled every five years; libraries groan with the weight of new books...In fact, our generation possesses more data about the universe and human personality than all previous generations put together. High school graduates today have been exposed to more information about the world than Plato, Aristotle, Spinoza, or Benjamin Franklin. In terms of facts alone, neither Moses nor Paul could pass a college entrance exam today.
>
> Yet, by everyone's standards, even with all our knowledge...society today is peopled with a bumper crop of brilliant failures...men and women educated to earn a living often don't know anything about handling life itself. Alumni from noted universities have mastered information about a narrow slice of life, but couldn't make it out of the first grade when it comes to living successfully with family and friends. Let's face it. Knowledge is not enough to meet life's problems. We need wisdom, the ability to handle life with skill.[13]

If our generation has learned anything, it should have learned by now that knowledge is no substitute for wisdom. Pastor Charles Spurgeon once said, "Wisdom is the right use of knowledge. To know is not to be wise. Many men know a great deal and are all the greater fools for it. There is no fool so great a fool as a knowing fool; but to know how to use knowledge is to have wisdom."[14]

I've got great news for all of us dads—the wisdom we need is abundantly available, and we can find it if we seek it. Solomon said in Proverbs 2:3-5:

> Indeed, if you call out for insight
>   and cry aloud for understanding,
> and if you look for it as for silver
>   and search for it as for hidden treasure,
> then you will understand the fear of the Lord
>   and find the knowledge of God.

I repeat: Proverbs is God's treasure chest of heavenly wisdom. You don't have to look long to find it, and when you do find it, you don't have to unlock it. All you have to do is open it and enjoy the jewels of wisdom that are there.

Solomon compares wisdom to a cry that can be heard anywhere (1:20-21) and to a free meal that can be eaten at any time (9:1-6). So dad, understand up front—whether or not you avail yourself of God's wisdom, God's wisdom is available.

Wisdom: If You Want It, You Can Have It

Proverbs makes it abundantly clear that if you ask for wisdom, you will get wisdom. Based on that assurance, I offer here for every dad a fail-safe, foolproof formula for getting wisdom.

First, you must admit you need it. Benjamin Franklin rightly said, "The doorstep to the temple of wisdom is a knowledge of your own ignorance."[15]

Second, you must go to the right source, and the only infallible source of wisdom is God: "For the Lord gives wisdom."[16] Only God can give wisdom because only God has wisdom.

Not only does God have a monopoly on wisdom, but His wisdom makes our wisdom look like foolishness. Paul said that even "the *foolishness* of God is wiser than human wisdom."[17]

Think about that. If God were capable of a stupid thought, that thought would be wiser than the wisest thought a human being could ever conceive.[18]

The eternal Father knows more about how to raise children than all earthly fathers who have ever lived, put together. And God is not hoarding His wisdom; He is eager to give it away. "If any of you lacks wisdom, you should ask God, who gives generously to all without finding fault, and it will be given to you."[19] But you must ask for it. You fail to do so at your own peril.

As you probably know, professional golfers play with a caddie. The caddie is more than a carrier of clubs; he is there for support and valuable advice. Tommy Bolt was one of the greatest golfers of all time, but he had one major flaw—a volcanic temper. One year he was playing in a tournament in southern California, and he was still steaming because of a bad round the day before. He told his caddie only to say, "Yes, Mr. Bolt," or "No, Mr. Bolt," if he were asked a question. Otherwise, he was to keep silent.

Bolt hit his first tee shot, and it appeared to come to rest behind a tree. When they reached the spot, Bolt asked his caddie, "Do you think I should hit a five-iron?" The caddie simply replied, "No, Mr. Bolt." Bolt hit the five-iron anyway and made an unbelievable shot that landed on the green a few feet from the hole.

He turned to his caddie and proudly said, "What did you think about that shot?"

As the caddie picked up the bag and headed toward the green, he said, "It wasn't your ball, Mr. Bolt."[20] Better to ask for wisdom now than to look foolish later!

Wisdom: If You Get It, Use It

Wisdom is not some aloof professor sitting in an ivory tower, oblivious to the needs of the people below. Real wisdom wears shoe leather, overalls, drives a pickup truck, goes to the grocery store, paints houses, draws a paycheck, suffers in the hospital, and cries at the funeral home. Remember, wisdom is to be found "out in the open…in the public square…at the city gate."[21] Wisdom gets down to the nitty-gritty of life. It's where the action is.

Since this book is about helping your children make wise decisions, let me give you a working definition of wisdom: *Wisdom is seeing life through the eyes of God, and living life in the will of God.* Proverbs gives fathers the skills not only to be wise dads, but it also enables them to pass along the skills of wisdom to their children.

Proverbs deals with the five major areas of life: the financial, the emotional, the physical, the relational, and the spiritual. I think all of us dads would agree that if we can help our children be wise in those five areas, we will have done a good life's work. The rest of this book gives us principles of godly wisdom to enable our children to be successful in these five areas.

My wish for all of us dads is that we would turn back to the one Book that has the answers for all the problems our kids face, and that we would be godly enough and wise enough to pass along these answers to our children. That is what I want for my children and for yours too.

Dad, would you right now put down this book and pray this simple prayer with me? It's a prayer that, if said sincerely, can have dramatic and positive effects on your family for generations to come:

> *Lord, I need wisdom—wisdom to be the dad to my children that I know You want me to be. I humbly admit my ignorance, and I confidently ask that You would keep Your Word and give me daily the divine wisdom to be the kind of dad I need to be. I pledge, with Your help, to pass on godly wisdom to my children, and I thank You for hearing my prayer. In Jesus's name, amen.*

2

Learn to Discern Between Friends, Foes, and Fools

"I will pay more for the ability to deal with people than any other ability under the sun."

JOHN D. ROCKEFELLER

When my children were young, I was always careful to learn about the friends they were making. I wanted to know their parents, what kind of language they were using, and how mischievous they were. My kids perceived this as the habits of an overbearing parent, but it was more than that. It was the expression of a father who knew that relationships matter.

Almost every job I've ever held is the result of a personal connection I had with someone. Many of the people I've employed over the years were friends I made years ago. When life has proven blissful, I've been able to celebrate with friends. And when life dragged me through the mud, those same relationships sustained me. The people you establish and maintain friendships with will help determine the trajectory of your life.

What is true for adults is equally if not more true for our children. Relationships can make your child or break your child. According to Solomon, your children will encounter people of every sort along life's way. Some will become friends, others will become foes (even Jesus had enemies), and others will prove themselves to be fools. You do your children an incredible favor by teaching them both how to differentiate between these groups of people and how to relate to them with wisdom and personal skill.

> As your children begin this long journey called life, one of the great treasures you can help them find is true friendship.

Early on, our children need to learn how rare and valuable true friendship is. Most of us make very few true friends in life, and Solomon warns us that not every so-called friend will prove to be one: "One who has unreliable friends soon comes to ruin."[1] The wrong "friend" may betray you—as Judas proved with Jesus. But a true friend may save your life—as Jonathan proved with David. So as your children begin this long journey called life, one of the great treasures you can help them find is true friendship. Thankfully, Proverbs contains a treasure trove of divine wisdom in this area.

Let's Be Friends

Solomon said, "A man who has friends must himself be friendly."[2] If you want to have a friend, you must first be a friend. One unknown poet expresses it this way:

> I went out to find a friend
> but could not find one there;
> I went out to be a friend,
> and friends were everywhere.

Friendliness does not have to be limited by personality. It does not necessarily mean having an aggressive, dynamic personality, getting in everyone's face, and slapping them on the back, with words flowing ninety miles a minute. Even the shy, quiet, and reserved person can learn to be friendly. You do not *take* friends; you *make* friends. So the best way to find a good friend is to be a good friend. It is next to impossible to have friends if you aren't friendly. The opposite is also true.

Psychologists once asked a group of college students to jot down the initials of the people they disliked. Some of the students taking the test could think of only one person; others listed as many as fourteen. But the interesting fact that came out of the research was this: Those who disliked the largest number of people were themselves the most widely disliked.[3] You will find that the more likable you are, the more likely you are to like other people and to be liked by them.

One of the greatest lessons I have ever learned on how to be a friend came from Dale Carnegie, the author of the bestseller *How to Win Friends and Influence People*. He said, "You can make more friends in two months by becoming interested in other people, than you can in two years by trying to get other people interested in you."

Being friendly is both a science and an art. It can be learned and improved with practice. That's why I taught my children to follow these practical guidelines:

- Maintain eye contact. When you talk to people, look them in the eye, not at your shoes.

- Smile. It's amazing how a simple smile can change the course of a conversation.

- Call people by their names. Strangers are just that, strange, but a friend is known.

- Learn to ask questions. You can make friends more easily if you learn to discuss everyone's favorite topic: themselves.

- Be kind. Find occasion to give a word of encouragement or to offer a compliment.

Show me a person who practices and applies those five traits with whomever he comes in contact, and I will show you a person who has a reputation for being friendly.

> "Be friendly to everyone,
> but don't have everyone as a friend."

Choose Wisely

A good rule of thumb on friendship is "Be friendly to everyone, but don't have everyone as a friend." Dad, urge your kids to heed Solomon's warning: "The righteous choose their friends carefully, but the way of the wicked leads them astray."[4] The Hebrew word translated *choose* can mean "to spy out; to examine," and is used in the Old Testament of a man searching out land. The wise person explores and evaluates prospective friendships, selects them prudently, and enters into them carefully.

Benjamin Franklin once said, "Be slow in choosing a friend, and even slower in changing." That is excellent advice. It is important not only to choose friends but to reject the wrong friends. One should choose his friends carefully because "the way of the wicked leads them astray."

Our jails are filled with convicts who should have been college graduates contributing to society; instead, they ran with the wrong crowd. Mark it down: Listening to the wrong people, following the wrong advice, and emulating the wrong example is the sure result of wrong friendships.

It is a truism that you can never be at the right place, at the right time, doing the right thing if you are with the wrong crowd. Part of our responsibilities as dads is to help our kids run with the right crowd. But just how involved and how strict a role should dads play in the friendships our kids make and the company they keep?

I was reared in a home where my dad had one rule: As long as I put my feet under his table, ate his food, slept under his roof, and lived in his house, *he* set the rules. I had clear guidelines of what was expected of me in terms of respect, work, grades, and the type of friends I could have. When I became a dad, I had basically the same policy, and my sons understood it.

> There are two superglue qualities that can permanently cement any friendship: *honesty* and *loyalty*.

As children get older and show good judgment, they should naturally be given more liberty to make their own decisions about an increasing number of things, including friendships. Yet my wife and I were involved in those choices and used the following guidelines to monitor our kids' close friends:

Understand the difference between your kids' acquaintances and those friends who are within their spheres of influence. Your child will gravitate toward certain kids for various reasons. These are the kids they hang with, talk to on the phone, invite to the house, sit with in church, and so forth. Since you cannot monitor every relationship your child has, make sure you know who these influential friends are.

As much as possible, make and take opportunities to get to know these friends personally. Through the years, we have made arrangements for all three of our sons to have their friends over, whether to play, spend the night, or just hang out. I find out all I can about them, asking questions about their church attendance, parents, and, if they are old enough, their relationship to Christ. I observe the way they talk, dress, show respect (or don't), and the way they play and interact with my family.

If my son is invited to a friend's house, I meet the parents, find out what activity might be planned outside the home, and make sure there is going to be adequate supervision. I assure the parents that my son will conduct himself as a Christian and show courtesy and respect. I also ask that they inform me if there is a problem of any kind.

I watch for any signs that my child is running with the wrong crowd. These signs include a loss of interest in spiritual things or an openly rebellious spirit.

Keeping Good Friends Close

Once you find a true friend, guard that relationship as you would the gold at Fort Knox. I believe there are two superglue qualities that can permanently cement any friendship: *honesty* and *loyalty.*

Proverbs 27:6 reminds us, "Wounds from a friend can be trusted, but an enemy multiplies kisses." A real friend may wound you by telling you the truth, but he will tell you the truth nonetheless. A real friend may not always tell you what you want to hear, but he will always tell you what you need to hear. In the short run it may hurt you, but in the long run it will help you.

If you would like to measure a relationship to determine whether it qualifies as a genuine friendship, here are two questions to ask yourself:

- Can I trust this person to be totally honest with me?
- Can I trust this person enough to be totally honest with him or her?

Only a true friendship expects, and can survive, mutual honesty.

The other quality involved in keeping a friend is *loyalty.* Solomon said, "There is a friend who sticks closer than a brother."[5] This is a poignant picture of just how close-knit one friend should be to another. Loyalty is one thing a person should never have to question about his friend. A true friend will always be your defense attorney before he becomes your judge.

There is no such thing as a fair-weather friend. You don't need friends in fair weather; you need them when it gets nasty! When life claws at you and you want to give up. A fair-weather friend is truly no friend at all.

I've read several definitions of a friend, but one of the most humorous comes from the late Erma Bombeck: "A friend is somebody who won't go on a diet when you're fat." I offered my children one that's a bit more helpful: A friend is someone who will walk into your house when the whole world has just walked out.

On one occasion, I had the privilege of being with the late Charles Colson. Colson was known as President Richard Nixon's "hatchet man" before Watergate and spent some time in prison for his part in the cover-up. Through the trauma of his experiences, Colson became a Christian and later wrote the bestseller *Born Again.* In the book he told how he was invited to speak at a university soon after his release from prison. The public was still hostile toward those involved in Watergate, especially Richard Nixon.

The students fired increasingly antagonistic questions at Colson. One student finally referenced some vicious criticism that

Henry Kissinger had leveled at Richard Nixon. "Mr. Colson," he demanded, "do you agree with this criticism?"

Colson said he scanned the room and could tell every ear was waiting to hear what he would say. "We all know Mr. Nixon's negative qualities. He has been dissected in the press like no one in history," Colson said. "I could tell you his good points, but I don't believe I could persuade you to accept them. But what it comes down to is, no, I don't go along with Henry Kissinger's comments. Mr. Nixon is my friend, and I don't turn my back on my friends."[6]

Colson said for a moment he thought the roof would fall in, and in a way, it did. But not as he expected. A moment of silence was followed by a thunderous, standing ovation. Even hostile students could appreciate the loyalty of a friend.

> If you ever want to find out who your friends
> really are, just make a mistake. Many of those you
> thought were friends will desert you like
> rats on a sinking ship.

If you ever want to find out who your friends really are, just make a mistake. Many of those you thought were friends will desert you like rats on a sinking ship. The true ones will stay. So Solomon admonished in Proverbs 27:10, "Do not forsake your friend or a friend of your family."

Loving Those Who Dislike You

Your children need to know that they will make foes as well as friends. That's part of life. The question is not, *will your kids make enemies* but rather *how will they respond to them*? Friends can bring out the best in us, but oh, how our foes can bring out the worst. Solomon passed two words of counsel along to his children concerning their foes.

First, frame them with forgiveness. Solomon said:

> Do not gloat when your enemy falls;
>   when they stumble, do not let your heart rejoice,
> or the Lord will see and disapprove
>   and turn his wrath away from them.
> Do not fret because of evildoers
>   or be envious of the wicked,
> for the evildoer has no future hope,
>   and the lamp of the wicked will be snuffed out.[7]

Don't allow the cancer of bitterness to destroy you; it is better to take your medicine now than to agonize later. Therefore, *never wish ill on your enemy; leave revenge to God.* God can handle your foes and punish them far better than you ever could. When you try to take matters into your own hands, you not only dam up God's anger, but you hold back His vengeance.

Revenge is God's business, not ours. Paul put the matter succinctly, yet firmly, when he said, "Do not take revenge, my dear friends, but leave room for God's wrath, for it is written: 'It is mine to avenge; I will repay,' says the Lord."[8]

The question is not, *will your kids make enemies* but rather *how will they respond to them?*

No "friend" in history was more guilty of betrayal than Judas Iscariot. He sided with the bitterest foes Jesus had, yet Jesus loved him to the very end. I know that the famous humorist Will Rogers said he never met a man he didn't like, but that is only because he didn't live long enough to meet some people I have! Your children should know that God has not called us to *like* everybody, but He has called us to *love* everybody.

Second, kill them with kindness. It's not enough merely to leave your enemies alone. We must be proactive and demonstrate love to them. Solomon said in Proverbs 25:21-22:

> If your enemy is hungry, give him food to eat;
>   if he is thirsty, give him water to drink.
> In doing this, you will heap burning coals on his head,
>   and the LORD will reward you.

Is your enemy hungry? Then cook him a hot meal. Is your enemy thirsty? Then give him a glass of homemade, ice-cold lemonade. The result? You will "heap burning coals on his head." What does this mean? The imagery of burning coals represents pangs of conscience, brought about more effectively by kindness rather than by violence. These "coals of kindness" produce the sharp pain of remorse and regret, which may lead to repentance.[9] Charles Swindoll offers additional insight into the possible origins of this image:

> In ancient days, homes were heated and meals were fixed on a small portable stove, somewhat like our outside barbecue grills. Frequently, a person would run low on hot coals and would need to replenish his supply. The container was commonly carried on the head. So, as the individual passed beneath second-story windows, thoughtful people who had extra hot coals in their possession would reach out of the window and place them in the container atop his head. Thanks to the thoughtful generosity of a few folks, he would arrive at the site with a pile of burning coals on his head, and a ready-made fire for cooking and keeping warm. "Heaping burning coals on someone's head" came to be a popular expression for a spontaneous and courteous act one person would voluntarily do for another.[10]

> The best way to defeat your enemy
> is to make a friend of him.

Truly, the best way to defeat your enemy is to make a friend of him. So teach your children, and remember yourself, that you are never more like Jesus than when you return good for evil and love your enemies.

Years ago, a man in my church got angry with me over a situation I had to handle not long after I came there as pastor. He confronted me after one service and then left. I thought he would not return but he did—angrier than ever. I was not in the wrong for what had transpired, but he was convinced I was.

Each Sunday he would attend church, sit toward the front, fold his arms, and put on his bless-me-if-you-can face. I dreaded seeing him each Sunday and even began to pray that he would stop coming. Then the Lord reminded me that there were two things my adversary could not fight: my prayers and my love.

I decided to change my tactics, making a conscious effort to speak to him and almost forcing him to shake my hand. I would affirm his presence whenever I saw him, but nothing changed. His response did not deter me; I kept praying and loving him as much as he'd let me.

Almost two years later, my assistant informed me that this man had come to meet with me. When he entered my office, I knew something was radically different. He said, "Hello, Pastor" (he had never called me anything, especially that). No sooner had the door shut than he began to weep and said, "Pastor, I was wrong in the way I have treated you. I have come to ask for your forgiveness." I embraced him and informed him that he had already been forgiven, and we forged a strong friendship that day.

Over the next several years, we drew closer, and he and his wife even took a trip with my family.

The story reminds me of Edwin Markham's beautiful poem:

> He drew a circle that shut me out—
> Heretic, rebel, a thing to flout.
> But love and I had the wit to win:
> We drew a circle that took him in.

Beware the Fool

Solomon talks often about another type of person everyone encounters: the fool. Three Hebrew words are used to describe this person in Proverbs. One word refers to a hardheaded person who thinks he needs no advice. Another term suggests a thick-headed person who refuses to listen to counsel. And the third term depicts an empty-headed person who carries out his lack of wisdom in a foolish lifestyle.

The fool is an empty-headed, thickheaded, or hardheaded person who gets an *F* in the school of wisdom. This obstinate man or woman may be intellectually brilliant, financially successful, and socially admired, but they are morally and spiritually bankrupt. Solomon warns us early on about fools. In the very first chapter he says, "The fear of the LORD is the beginning of knowledge, but fools despise wisdom and instruction."[11]

Rather than list every verse in Proverbs that describes the fool, I have noted the categories of people Proverbs marks as fools. It would be a good exercise for you to go over this list with your children to see if they know anyone who fits one of these categories. A fool is:

- the loud mouth who loves to hear himself talk, and forces others to do the same (18:2)

- the hot-tempered bully who thinks anger, violence, and the bigger gun proves his worth (12:16; 14:16)

- the pseudo-intellectual who thinks he knows more than God (26:7,9)

- the know-it-all who thinks what he doesn't know isn't worth learning (12:15a; 26:12). The fool is often wrong but never in doubt!

- the rebellious child or teenager who loves evil, hates good, and thinks sin is a joke (10:23; 13:19)

- the impulsive talker who *always* lets you know what's on his mind and is willing to give you a piece of it even when there is none to spare (17:27-28)

- the ladder-climber who puts wealth, position, and material possessions above the happiness and well-being of his family (11:29)

- the divisive troublemaker who loves to start arguments (20:3)

- the wasteful spendthrift who blows money faster than he earns it and saves nothing (21:20)

- the self-confident person who trusts his own heart, mind, and judgment rather than the God who gave him all three (19:3; 28:25-26)

- the gossip who spreads slander, lies, and half-truths, not caring who it hurts. Usually he has enough cowardice to talk about a person but not enough courage to talk to the person (10:18).

- the hardheaded child or teenager who hates the wise instruction of a godly father and breaks the heart of a godly mother (10:1; 15:5)

- the stubborn sinner who never learns from his mistakes and keeps doing the same thing repeatedly while expecting different results (26:11-12)

One of the reasons Solomon wanted to instill wisdom in the hearts of his children was to keep them away from these types of persons so his children would not become fools themselves. Solomon knew that "fools die for lack of sense."[12] Just as the body will die from lack of oxygen, a person can die from a lack of wisdom. They can kill friendships, job opportunities, and even their reputation.

How does Solomon think your son or daughter should relate to fools? By saturating his or her presence with their absence. He says, "Stay away from a fool, for you will not find knowledge on their lips."[13] According to the wise king, only a fool fools around with fools!

One of the most valuable lessons you can teach your children is how to evaluate potential friends. The following list of questions can help your children to determine who should be included in that special circle called friends—questions you should ask of their friends as well.

- *Does this person profess to follow Christ?* This does not mean that your children cannot associate with non-Christians, but rather that your child, and you, should do all you can to influence them for Christ rather than be influenced by their unChristlike behaviors.[14]

- *Does this person draw me closer to God or farther from Him?*[15]

- *What kind of company does this person keep?*[16]

- *Does this person try to involve me in questionable or unhealthy activities?*[17]

- *Does this person show respect to their parents?* Always observe a potential friend's relationship to their family.[18]

- *Does this person try to control their tongue?* A person's speech reveals much about their heart.[19]

- *Does this person have a violent temper or do they exercise reasonable self-control?*[20]

- *Does this person have a positive attitude or a negative one?*[21]

- *Is this person trustworthy and honest?* Look for friends that are loyal and true.[22]

> Dad, the best person to teach your child about relationships—and especially about friendship— is you. When you get right down to it, *friendship is what fatherhood is all about.*

Dad, these are just a few questions you and your children might ask, not only about others to evaluate their friendships, but also about themselves to evaluate their own worth as a friend. Again, one cannot be too careful in choosing one's friends.

Become Your Child's Best Friend

Taped to the bookshelf in my study (where I can see it from my desk every day) is a letter to me from my youngest son, Joshua. He wrote it one month before his tenth birthday. I read it nearly every day:

> *I love you, Dad. I will never forget you. You are the greatest dad ever. Words can't express my thoughts about you. I love you more than anything. You are my very best friend.*

The whole time I was at school today I was thinking about you and wanting to be with you. At home when you prayed with me I had the greatest day ever.

I love you,
Joshua Merritt

What kind of friendship do you have with your children? Dad, the best person to teach your child about relationships—and especially about friendship—is you. Why not show your children what a friend is by being their very best friend? When you get right down to it, *friendship is what fatherhood is all about.* You *can* be your child's best friend.

Though my three sons are now grown and on their own, I still remind them, "You are my best friend." To hear them say, "You are my best friend too, Dad," still sets my heart on fire and makes me grateful that God allowed me to father the greatest sons in the world.

One episode of the ever-classic *Andy Griffith Show* pictures fatherhood at its finest. Young Opie comes into his father Andy's office after a trip into the woods breathless and excited. He said, "Pa, I saw a man who walked on the trees!" Andy thought the wild story was the product of a vivid imagination. His deputy sidekick, Barney, the quintessential know-it-all, insisted that Opie be spanked for lying.

Opie made another trip to the woods and returned with the same story and added the name of the tree walker. Andy was disgusted with Opie's insistence, but he refused to inflict any punishment. Barney said, "Andy, you don't believe that tall tale, do you?" Andy replied, "No, I don't, but I do believe in Opie."[23]

Even when you struggle with the developing character of your children, make sure they always know you believe in *them*. And show them how much you believe in them and care for them by teaching them how to discern between friends, foes, and fools. This may be the greatest gift you can give them for it will outlive you by generations.

It Doesn't Take Much to Say a Lot

"I've never been hurt by anything I didn't say."

CALVIN COOLIDGE,
THIRTIETH PRESIDENT OF THE UNITED STATES

It wasn't long before my first son began to grow and develop. I blinked and he was turning himself over. Then crawling. And finally, walking. One afternoon, he tugged on my pant leg and pulled himself up. Then he looked me in the face and said, "Dada." I nearly fell out of my chair.

Looking back, maybe he was just cooing. After all, he didn't say anything again for some time. But you couldn't have convinced me of that in the moment. I was sure of it. He'd said my name.

It wouldn't be long until his vocabulary began to expand. He'd learn to ask for food and scream no at the top of his lungs. Those toddler years were a roller coaster of affirmation and anguish. Every word had the power to lift my spirits or crush them.

What we learn from our children in their first years proves all the more true later in life. Words are powerful. And the tongue can serve as both a destructive weapon and a healing balm.

Almost one hundred years ago the following statement was made, and it is as true today as it was then:

There is nothing which seems more insubstantial than speech, a mere vibration in the atmosphere which touches the nerves of hearing and then dies away. There is no organ which seems smaller and less considerable than the tongue; a little member which is not even seen, and physically speaking, soft and weak. But the word which issues out of the lips is the greatest power in human life.[1]

Only one man in the history of America ever resigned from the presidency. Have you ever considered what really brought Richard Nixon down? Conventional thinking said it was the tapes of his private conversations. But it was not the tapes; it was his tongue. It was not the tapes but *what he said on the tapes* that sealed his doom.

> The average person speaks enough
> in a lifetime to make twelve thousand volumes
> of three hundred pages each.

Never underestimate the awesome power of the spoken word. For every word in Adolf Hitler's book, *Mein Kampf,* 125 people died in World War II.[2]

Consider this: the average person speaks enough in a lifetime to make twelve thousand volumes of three hundred pages each. If that is the average, think about the substantial libraries many of us are leaving behind!

Solomon was also concerned that his children be wise in the way they used their tongues. He made this strong statement about that little organ that lies behind our teeth: "The tongue has the power of life and death, and those who love it will eat its fruit."[3]

The ancient king had much to say about what comes out of our mouths. The words *tongue, mouth, lips,* and *words* are mentioned in Proverbs almost 150 times. Solomon's emphasis on our words tells us that we had better take care of the sounds that flow from our mouths. And we do well as dads to teach our kids the same principle.

> Even a small number of words can determine the fabric and destiny of the lives of your children.

It's Not Quantity, It's Quality That Counts

My son's words had power in my life before he could barely string together a sentence. In the same way, even a small number of words can determine the fabric and destiny of the lives of your children. Consider this:

- "I love you." These words can lead to engagement.
- "Will you marry me?" These words can lead to a life-time commitment.
- "Let's start a family." These words can bring forth children and grandchildren.
- "I've decided to major in…" These words can determine a lifelong vocation.
- "Yes." This word spoken to Jesus Christ can open the door to eternity with God.

Solomon gave us a specific reason why he desired a heart of wisdom for his children:

> My son, if your heart is wise,
>   then my heart will be glad indeed;
> my inmost being will rejoice
>   when your lips speak what is right.[4]

With their hearts, Solomon wanted his children to think wisely. With their hands, Solomon wanted his children to do wisely. But with their lips, Solomon wanted his children to speak wisely. A little ditty by William E. Norris I heard years ago perfectly summarizes what Solomon is telling us and our children:

> If your lips you would keep from slips,
> Five things observe with care:
> To whom you speak; of whom you speak;
> And how, and when, and where.

Remember, dad, we are living in an age where saying the wrong thing can get you sued or shot. This has never been more true than in the age of Twitter and texting. You will be hard-pressed to find a greater life lesson to teach your children than how to control their tongues.

> The less we think, the more we speak,
> and the quicker we say it,
> the more likely we are to get into trouble.

Don't Eat Your Words

One verse especially encapsulates Solomon's philosophy about human speech and the central lesson he wanted his children to learn: "Those who guard their lips preserve their lives, but those who speak rashly will come to ruin."[5] The less we think, the more we speak, and the quicker we say it, the more likely we are to get into trouble.

Unfortunately, many times we get into the situation of the vacuum cleaner salesman who had been assigned a backwoods, rural area for his territory. He was going from farmhouse to farmhouse on his first day on the job, trying to sell vacuum cleaners. As he approached one farmhouse, he knocked on the door and was met by a farmer's wife who asked him what he wanted.

Without asking permission, he barged right past her into the kitchen and said, "I'm selling vacuum cleaners."

"Wait a minute," she said.

"Ma'am, before you say anything, I want to show you something."

"But—"

"Watch this!" He reached into his bag, pulled out a bucket of dirt, and threw it all over her wooden floor. "If my vacuum cleaner won't pick up all that dirt, I'll eat it!"

"Then you better get busy," she said, "'cause we don't have any electricity."

> Teach your kids early and often to guard the words that come out of their mouths. They are conduits of life and death, encouragement and distraction, healing and hurting.

How often we have to eat the words we so carelessly throw about. Teach your kids early and often to guard the words that come out of their mouths. They are conduits of life and death, encouragement and distraction, healing and hurting. Teach them to watch their words, for they never know which ones they'll have to eat.

Proverbs also issues stern warnings to the gossip, to the loose cannon, to the person who indiscriminately spreads rumors like wildfire. Solomon repeatedly warned his children about being involved in gossip, either on the giving end or on the receiving end. On the one hand, he warned about the one who gossips:

A gossip betrays a confidence,
   but a trustworthy person keeps a secret.[6]

A perverse person stirs up conflict,
   and a gossip separates close friends.[7]

> Gossip is damaged goods sold at a premium price,
> spoiling both the seller and the buyer.

The word *gossip* comes from a Hebrew word that means "to go about" and is probably derived from a word meaning "merchant."[8] A gossip, then, is someone who goes about peddling tales. I define *gossip* as "a false or unverified negative report about another person discussed with a third party with the intent to do harm." Gossip is damaged goods sold at a premium price, spoiling both the seller and the buyer.

People cannot be judged by what others say about them, but they can be judged by what they say about others. This is a great lesson all of us dads could teach our kids. What are you modeling for your children by what you say about others? Do you use your words to tear down or to build up? Don't fool yourself; your kids are listening and learning.

The ant lion, more popularly known as the doodlebug, lives at the bottom of a little cone-shaped hole he burrows in the sand. He gets down as low as possible into that cone so he's always looking up at everything else. When an ant comes around and gets on the side of this carefully prepared cone, the doodlebug feels a few grains of sand slide down, which signals him that food has arrived. Then the doodlebug begins to throw dirt on his victim, trying to drag that ant down to his level. This is what we do when we gossip—we throw dirt on others, hoping to bring them down to our level.

That's why Solomon warned against being not only a gossip-bearer but also a gossip-hearer. This lesson is so important that he repeated a proverb word-for-word in his book, something he did rarely. Proverbs 18:8 and 26:22 are identical: "The words of a gossip are like choice morsels; they go down to the inmost parts."

The ear craves gossip like a hungry stomach craves food. That's why Solomon goes on to give this warning: "A gossip betrays a confidence; so avoid anyone who talks too much."[9] Most kids will have one of two tendencies: either to have gossipy lips or gossipy ears. If they have gossipy lips, teach them not to share gossip. If they have gossipy ears, teach them not to receive it.

In most states it is illegal both to steal and to receive stolen goods. Similarly, the apostle Paul admonished, "Do not *receive* an accusation against an elder except from two or three witnesses."[10] Remember, the gossiper must always have an accomplice to commit the crime. Train up your child to be someone who doesn't sprinkle, spread, or have to eat the dirt of their words.

> The potential for saying the wrong thing increases proportionately to the number of words you say.

Less Is Always Better than More

"In the multitude of words sin is not lacking, but he who restrains his lips is wise."[11] This is not only a law of speech, but also a law of science. I think it can be proven that your odds of putting your foot in your mouth increase the more times you open it. Put another way, the potential for saying the wrong thing increases proportionately to the number of words you say.

Have you ever noticed that the person who is always putting in his two cents' worth usually says something that is worth about two cents? I read something recently that gave me pause. It said, "He who thinks by the inch and speaks by the yard should be kicked by the foot." I could put it this way: When you open your lips, don't shoot from the hips, or you'll shoot yourself in the behind.

Only a fool speaks rashly and recklessly. Indeed, a person who is hasty in his words is worse than a fool. Solomon recorded this sage observation: "Do you see someone who speaks in haste? There is more hope for a fool than for them."[12] When it comes to our words, haste makes waste.

Solomon never forgot his own advice, even as an old man. In Ecclesiastes 5:2 he would later write,

> Do not be quick with your mouth,
>   do not be hasty in your heart
>   to utter anything before God.
> God is in heaven
>   and you are on earth,
>   so let your words be few.

A wealthy grandfather was getting up in age. Because he was going deaf he went to the doctor and was fitted with a unique hearing aid. It not only overcame the old man's deafness and allowed him to hear perfectly, but it was concealed so no one could see it.

When he went back to the doctor for a checkup, the doctor said, "Your family must be extremely happy to know that you can now hear." The grandfather said, "Well, I haven't told them about my hearing aid. I just sit around and listen to the conversations. I've already changed my will three times."

You never know who is listening, but you can know that your words are having an impact. So let your words be few and teach your children to do the same.

Flatter Me Not

Everyone is susceptible to flattery. We all love to have our egos stroked and hear how wonderful we are. I am convinced that most one-night stands and adulterous liaisons begin with a single flattering comment. Listen to Eugene Peterson's unique translation of Proverbs 29:5 (MSG): "A flattering neighbor is up to no good; he's probably planning to take advantage of you."

> A flatterer is someone who will pat you on the shoulder with one hand and knife you in the back with the other.

Beware of flatterers. In the long run, Solomon says, you are better off with a person who will criticize you than one who will flatter you. "Whoever rebukes a person will in the end gain favor rather than one who has a flattering tongue."[13]

A flatterer is someone who will pat you on the shoulder with one hand and knife you in the back with the other. Flattery is something a person will say to your face but will not say behind your back. It is insincere praise from an insincere motive.

We can teach our children three wonderful lessons about the fine line between praise and flattery (and the best way to teach them is to remember to keep from crossing that line ourselves):

- *Lesson 1*: Teach your children to give praise sparingly but sincerely, with nothing but the best in mind for the other person.

- *Lesson 2*: Teach your children to receive praise wisely, without taking either themselves or the person giving the praise too seriously.

- *Lesson 3*: Know the difference between insincere

> flattery and sincere praise. Flattery is what someone
> will say to your face but not behind your back. Praise
> is what someone will say behind your back.

King Solomon reminded his children, "The crucible for silver and the furnace for gold, but people are tested by their praise."[14] A question we should always ask ourselves when we are praised is: Does this make me more bighearted or more bigheaded? Words test both the mouth that speaks them and the ears that hear them.

Be Profound, Not Profane

I don't think I have to tell any father that our society is growing increasingly coarse. Songs are riddled with vulgarities, talk radio and cable news is filled with name-calling, and almost everyone seems to believe that profanity is no longer profane. One thing we never tolerated in our home when my kids were growing up was profanity.

You can tell what kind of effect you're having on your children in their training and discipline by the words they use, especially when they get angry. Listen to these two statements, back to back:

> The heart of the righteous weighs its answers,
>   but the mouth of the wicked gushes evil.[15]

> The lips of the righteous know what finds favor,
>   but the mouth of the wicked only what is perverse.[16]

The first statement tells us that a wise person will think before he speaks because he realizes every word has a consequence. The second, that the lips of a righteous person know what is acceptable to say and remember that God hears every word.

When George H.W. Bush was running for president in 1988, he admitted that he had made inappropriate remarks about Dan Rather and CBS White House correspondent Leslie Stall after an on-the-air confrontation. Bush referred to Rather in an unprintable term and also took God's name in vain in speaking about CBS. When confronted with what he had said, he replied, "If I had known the microphone was on, I would not have taken the Lord's name in vain, and I apologize for that. I didn't know I was being taped, or I wouldn't have done it."[17]

But who we are when we think the microphone is off is a greater test of our true character. The president shouldn't have said it whether the tape was running or not. Remember, God's tape is always running. "For your ways are in full view of the LORD, and he examines all your paths."[18]

Later Jesus Himself declared, "There is nothing concealed that will not be disclosed, or hidden that will not be made known. What you have said in the dark will be heard in the daylight, and what you have whispered in the ear in the inner rooms will be proclaimed from the roofs."[19]

Dad, I urge you, teach your children about the value of intelligent, life-giving, and wholesome speech. Do this first by modeling and second by instructing. They will mimic the way you talk, so be the high standard-bearer you can and should be.

The Gold Standard

Solomon compared wise words, spoken in a timely fashion, to gold and silver.

> Like apples of gold in settings of silver
> is a ruling rightly given.
> Like an earring of gold or an ornament of fine gold
> is the rebuke of a wise judge to a listening ear.[20]

One mark of wisdom is the ability to say the right thing, in the right way, at the right time, to the right person—or not to say anything at all. One saying not found in Proverbs still contains powerful truth: "As a man grows wiser he talks less and says more."

Keep in mind that the key to the tongue is the heart. That is why Solomon said in Proverbs 18:4, "The words of the mouth are deep waters, but the fountain of wisdom is a rushing stream." "Deep waters" refers to the water at the bottom of the well that is the cleanest and the coldest.

If you want to know what kind of water a well really has, go down to the bottom to get it. If you want to know what is in a person's heart, listen to their words. The mouth is like an overflow pipe. It reveals not only what is in the heart but what *fills* the heart. Every time we speak, we raise the curtain of our hearts, exposing what it is really like.[21] Again, one of the benefits of instilling wisdom early on in the heart of your children is the purifying and sanctifying effect it has on their words.

As my children began to hear the wrong kinds of words at school, they brought them home, usually in the form of a question: "Daddy, what does _____ mean?" I always answered the question with another question: "Have you ever heard Daddy use this word?" I'm glad I can say the answer was no. I would then proceed to tell them not only why that word was inappropriate, but how God hears every word we say and holds us accountable for all of them.

I will never forget the time our family was out together and we heard a man nearby use a profane word. I believe it was Jonathan who said, *"We* don't talk like that, do we, Daddy?" Sweet words about dirty words, wouldn't you say?

Our instruction to our children must continuously be to their hearts as well as to their heads. When their hearts are right, what they speak will be right. The tongue is a barometer not only of physical health but also of spiritual health. We can glean three life lessons to teach our children about the wise use of their tongues:

First, use the tongue *cautiously*. One of the most groundbreaking, far-reaching judicial opinions ever handed down by the

Supreme Court was the *Miranda* decision. That opinion determined that every criminal suspect had a constitutional right to be advised of the availability of counsel. Part of what police are required to tell suspects under *Miranda* reads, "You have the right to remain silent. Anything you say can, and will, be used against you."

We ought to exercise that right in everyday living far more often than we do. Sometimes the wisest words are the ones never spoken. I don't know who said this, but I agree with it: "A wise man is one who thinks twice before saying nothing." Would you like for people to think you are smarter than you really are, rather than discover that you are dumber than they thought you were?

> The one who has knowledge uses words with restraint,
>   and whoever has understanding is even-tempered.
> Even fools are thought wise if they keep silent,
>   and discerning if they hold their tongues.[22]

It is better to keep your mouth shut and let people think you're a fool than to open it and remove all doubt! I have learned, the hard way, that one minute of keeping my mouth shut is worth an hour of explanation.

My first job as a teenager was in a local department store called Dixie City. The manager was a Jewish man whose last name was Grooh. I made up a little ditty about "Grooh the Jew," and unbeknownst to me, it was overheard by Mr. Grooh himself. He was a kind gentleman, and rather than fire me, he let it slide. Another employee, however, told me that Mr. Grooh had overheard me singing my stupid little song.

It was hard, but I did the right thing. I went into his office, confessed, and asked his forgiveness. I had made up the song out of immaturity, but my racist remark was still wrong. I could tell from the look on his face that irreparable damage had been done and my Christian witness had been tarnished. I learned too late that when in doubt say nothing, for it sure beats saying the wrong something.

> You may be misquoted or falsely quoted,
> but it is better to have others try to prove you said
> something you did not say than to condemn you
> for something you did say.

One of the most underrated presidents of all time was Calvin Coolidge. He was known as Silent Cal because he spoke very little. He never missed a chance to say little or nothing. Once he was sitting at a state dinner across from a young socialite, and she said, "Mr. President, I have a $100 bet [a sizable sum in the 1920s] that I can make you say at least three words." Without missing a beat or cracking a smile, he responded, "You lose." And she did!

The reverse of *Miranda* is also true: "What you *don't* say *can't* and *won't* be used against you." You may be misquoted or falsely quoted, but it is better to have others try to prove you said something you did not say than to condemn you for something you did say.

Second, use the tongue *carefully.* Solomon not only condemns the tongue that starts gossip; he also praises the tongue that stops gossip.

> A gossip betrays a confidence,
>   but a trustworthy person keeps a secret.[23]

> Whoever would foster love covers over an offense,
>   but whoever repeats the matter separates close
>   friends.[24]

The tongue should be used as a gossip-stopper, not a gossip-starter. Teach your kids to ask four questions of anyone who wants to tell them a juicy piece of information about someone else. These are guaranteed gossip-stoppers:

- How do you know this is true? (If its truth cannot be verified, it should not be reported.)
- Is this confidential? (If it is, the conversation is over.)
- Is it kind? (If it is not, why is the person sharing it?)
- Is it necessary? (If it is not, then talk about something else.)

Third, use the tongue *constructively.* One can hear or speak no greater word than an encouraging word. Solomon said, "Anxiety weighs down the heart, but a kind word cheers it up."[25] I have learned how vitally important encouragement is in the life of a family. Encouragement is like a peanut butter sandwich—the more you spread it around, the better things stick together.

My oldest son, James, played one year of Little League baseball when he was six years old. The entire season he did not as much as touch the ball as a batter—not even a foul tip! But what he carries with him to this day is the fact that I was always encouraging him, telling him how proud I was that he was standing up at the plate to face the pitchers with those twenty-mile-per-hour hummers coming at him. Not once did I yell, scream, or berate him for not hitting the ball. To this day he recalls my encouragement more than the discouragement of setting the all-time Little League whiff record.

The Royal British Navy has a regulation that reads, "No officer shall speak discouragingly to another officer in the discharge of his duties." How we need to practice that regulation in our homes!

Remember, it all starts with you. Do you want your kids to love God and live for Him? If so, use your tongue to teach your children early, consistently, and continuously the why and how of loving God. Another wise man named Moses gave this sage advice to parents a long time ago, but it is still priceless counsel today:

> Love the LORD your God with all your heart and with all your soul and with all your strength. These commandments that I give you today are to be on your hearts. Impress them on your children. Talk about them when you sit at home and when you walk along the road, when you lie down and when you get up.[26]

God gave us our tongues so that we might glorify Him. One of the best ways for us to do that is to teach our children to do likewise. A Sunday school teacher asked her first-grade class, "Why do you love God?" One little boy gave this classic answer: "I guess it just runs in our family."

Dad, that kind of love can run in *your* family if, guided by a heart of wisdom, your tongue speaks God's truth to your children. Words are so important to God that He spoke His truth through the greatest book ever written, the one we simply call "the Word." Teach your kids to keep that in mind when they speak. You'll be glad you did.

4

Lower Your Temper-ature

"When anger enters the mind, wisdom departs."

THOMAS À KEMPIS

Sometimes I wonder what it would be like to construct a time machine and relive my "daddy days." To hold my children again when their heads were no higher than my waist. To teach them all the lessons I've learned since they left home as adults. To avoid the many foolish mistakes I made. Unfortunately, parenting is like a lot of things: by the time you figure out the right way to do it, it's over.

> If I could go back in time and change only one thing from my fathering days, I know exactly what it would be. I would go back and die to my temper.

If I could go back in time, however, and change only one thing, I know exactly what it would be. I don't need time to think about it. I already have—on many sleepless nights and many restless mornings. I would go back and die to my temper. I would quiet my shouts, throw cold water on my fiery emotions, and remind myself to think before responding to my wife and children out of anger.

To be fair, I come by my temper honestly. My dad was a gruff "old South" man with a short fuse. He was ready to go fisticuffs with anyone who crossed him until the day he died of lung cancer. Living in his home taught me that a father needed to be firm, even feared. Along with a few other personality traits, my dad's temper got passed on to me. And no other flaw of mine caused more hurt and harm than this one.

Dad, take it from a father with the benefit of a few years: die to your temper. Avoid the shedding of unnecessary tears and the speaking of hurtful words. The pain is not worth it. And neither is the regret. Remember that *anger* is one letter short of danger. So learn to control your anger and teach your children to regulate theirs as well. It may spare you both from a boatload of grief and guilt down the road.

One of the most telling exercises you can undertake as a father is to ask your children the following two questions:

1. "What is my greatest strength as a father?"
2. "What is my greatest weakness as a father?"

I took the plunge many years ago and asked my two oldest sons these questions (separately), and I got identical responses. They both agreed on my greatest strength: "You have taught me about God—how to love Him and live for Him."

I must admit my big head swelled for a moment. But only for a moment. Because then they both answered the second question with lightning speed: "Your temper is your greatest weakness. You just don't have very much patience." That was almost twenty years ago. Oh, how I wish I had listened and learned to correct that problem then.

There's a Time to Be Angry

Moses, David, Jonah, and Peter (just to name a few biblical characters) all had one thing in common: They all got angry. Anger leaves tracks on the paths of life that are easy for anybody to find. One small spark of anger struck at the wrong time can start a raging fire that, in an instant, can consume a lifelong friendship. But there are also times when some level of anger is justified.

After all, anger is an emotion God Himself experiences. No less than eighteen times the Old Testament speaks of "the anger of the Lord." To those who want to emphasize the love of God exclusively against the holiness of God, Psalm 7:11 is a show-stopping verse: "God is a righteous judge, a God who displays his wrath every day." The word *wrath* in Hebrew literally means "to foam at the mouth." You have to be pretty mad to do that, but that is how God feels about wickedness.

Jesus was without sin, but He was not without anger. On one occasion He got angry when a man with a withered hand came to be healed on the Sabbath. The hypocritical Pharisees were watching to see if Jesus would perform what they thought was an ungodly act. We read in Mark 3:5, "[Jesus] looked around at them in anger."

Even God the Holy Spirit can be angry. First Samuel 11:6 tells us, "When Saul heard their words, the Spirit of God came powerfully upon him, and he burned with anger." It was the Spirit's presence in Saul that drove him to anger.

The secret to controlling one's temper is not to avoid anger but to vent one's anger rightly. Aristotle once said, "Anybody can become angry; that is easy. But to be angry with the right person, and to the right degree, and at the right time, and for the right purpose, and in the right way; that is not within everybody's power, and that is not easy."

Sometimes biblical characters got angry in the right way; at other times they didn't. When they allowed their temper to rage out of control, it produced devastating results. So we need to take a lesson from Solomon's father, David: "Be angry, and do not sin."[1]

At least two occasions made God angry, and they provide us lessons on when we ought to be angry. The first is when *God's people openly disobeyed Him.* Solomon never forgot a time when God got angry with him. The Bible records this incident in 1 Kings 11:9: "The LORD became angry with Solomon because his heart had turned away from the LORD, the God of Israel, who had appeared to him twice."

> When your children willfully, openly, defiantly rebel against you and your God-given authority, you *ought* to be angry, and you *ought* to channel that anger into constructive but loving correction.

Dads, we can learn a lesson here from God the Father. When your children willfully, openly, defiantly rebel against you and your God-given authority, you *ought* to be angry, and you *ought* to channel that anger into constructive but loving correction. Part of your job in rearing your children is to teach them how to control their anger, not how to eliminate it altogether.

Let's look at how Jesus got angry in this famous story:

> When it was almost time for the Jewish Passover, Jesus went up to Jerusalem. In the temple courts he found people selling cattle, sheep and doves, and others sitting at tables exchanging money. So he made a whip out of cords, and drove all from the temple courts, both sheep and cattle; he scattered the coins of the

money changers and overturned their tables. To those who sold doves he said, "Get these out of here! Stop turning my Father's house into a market!"[2]

Jesus was more than a little upset—He was *angry.* But He was angry

- at the *right place* (the temple, though anger at individuals should be privately expressed most of the time)
- at the *right people* (no problem with mistaken identity)
- for the *right reason* (over a wrong done to others—in this case, God)
- at the *right time* (the issue was dealt with immediately, though at times anger may be better expressed at another time so as to avoid humiliating someone)
- in the *right way* (in this case, a raised voice was necessary; at other times, it won't be)

Dad, early on when your child gets angry, use these five criteria to help your kids determine if their anger was appropriate under the circumstances. Teach them to express their anger only as a last resort, never in retaliation. And above all, remind them that Jesus got angry only when others were being wronged, not Himself.

The second occasion when God gets angry, and when we ought to as well, is when *people in authority and power stand for what is wrong and against what is right, and they hurt others in the process.* Listen to this scathing passage of Scripture that sounds as if it could have been written in the twentieth century:

> Woe to those who call evil good
>   and good evil,

who put darkness for light
and light for darkness,
who put bitter for sweet
and sweet for bitter.
Woe to those who are wise in their own eyes
and clever in their own sight.
Woe to those who are heroes at drinking wine
and champions at mixing drinks,
who acquit the guilty for a bribe,
but deny justice to the innocent...
Therefore the LORD's anger burns against his people;
his hand is raised and he strikes them down.
The mountains shake,
and the dead bodies are like refuse in the streets.
Yet for all this, his anger is not turned away,
his hand is still upraised.[3]

It is not wrong to be angry at wrong, particularly when that wrong is being done to someone else. *We ought to be angry:*

- Over the number of children suffering in the American foster care system and in orphanages around the globe.

- Over the millions of innocent, unborn babies whose lives are snuffed out each year by abortion.

- Over the millions of people who will die this year from hunger and contaminated water.

- Over cowardly politicians who do what is politically expedient instead of what is morally right, who protect the powerful and trample the poor.

- Over prejudice and injustice done to others because of the color of their skin or because of their gender.

Use this rule of thumb to help you gauge when anger is right and when it is wrong: *The way to be angry and not sin is to be angry at nothing but sin.* It is difficult but not impossible to be angry at wrong but not be wrong in your anger. Indeed, many of the problems in our culture today stem from a lack of righteous indignation.

Firewalls Needed

I am convinced that out of control tempers is one of the most destructive tumors growing on many American families today. A burning caldron of anger is running over in our society, spilling into our schools, our government, and even our homes. Consider this:

- More than 60 percent of the homicides in America are committed by angry family members.[4]

- The number one killer in America is heart disease. And one of the major causes of heart disease is anger. Dr. Redford Williams, director of Duke University's Behavioral Medicine Research Center, stated, "The hostility and anger associated with Type A behavior is the major contributor to heart disease in America."[5]

- People who struggle with anger are five times as likely to suffer coronary heart disease as the average person. People with heart disease more than double their risk of a heart attack when they get angry.[6]

Occasionally, we may become angry for a good reason, but usually it is an expression of our selfishness, impatience, irritation, or hurt over the way we have been treated.

Most every verse in Proverbs casts anger in a negative light because, most of the time, our anger is an expression of sin. Occasionally, we may become angry for a good reason, but usually it is an expression of our selfishness, impatience, irritation, or hurt over the way we have been treated.

When we look at the occasions when Jesus got angry—and there are only a few—we notice his anger is never directed at what someone did to *Him*. He never retaliated or lashed out at anyone who wronged Him. Even when His executioners nailed Him to the cross, He said, "Father, forgive them, for they do not know what they are doing."[7] Jesus grew angry only when *others* were hurt or wronged. So often our problem is just the opposite. We can get angry over someone hurting us, but we turn a deaf ear and a blind eye when others are being hurt.

Two boys walked into the dentist's office. One boy said, "Doc, we've got a lot of things we want to do today. We want to go outside and play; we don't want to spend all day in the dentist's office. I've got a tooth that's got to come out, and I want it to come out right now. Forget the Novocain and the painkillers, just get your pliers and pull it out."

"Well, son, I certainly do admire your courage," the dentist replied. "Which tooth is it?"

The boy turned to his buddy and said, "Show him your tooth, Tommy."

> The more self-centered we are,
> the more quick-tempered we will be.

Why is it that the pain we cause others affects us so little? Isn't it true that we too often get angry at things we shouldn't get angry over, while we don't get angry over things that should anger us?

I have learned that the more self-centered we are, the more quick-tempered we will be. It is that quick temper, the volcanic eruption that occurs when someone invades our territory, that is so dangerous.

The High Cost of a Hot Temper

I remember vividly my first trip to Israel. We flew into Amman, Jordan, and the next morning we visited Mount Nebo. As I stood on that plateau looking across the Jordan River to the fertile Jordan valley with its lush vegetation, verdant vineyards, and groves of banana trees, my mind went back to one of the greatest Jewish leaders ever—Moses.

Moses was a great leader and a meek man for the most part. But on one occasion, his anger got the best of him and caused him to disobey God. Because of his outburst, God prohibited Moses from entering the Promised Land. The closest he got was seeing it from Mount Nebo before he died.

Moses stood on that very same site, looking at a land flowing with milk and honey. I can hardly imagine how his heart ached to cross that Jordan River with his people and plant his feet on the sacred soil God had promised to Israel. He was oh so close yet so far away, and the invisible barrier that kept him out was his anger. One fitful moment cost Moses the opportunity he had spent his life waiting for.

Trust me, dad, your temper will rob you of many great opportunities if you don't learn to control it. I would give my eyes, arms, and legs to go back in time and father my children again without letting my temper get the best of me. Humorist Will Rogers was right: "People who fly into a rage seldom make a good landing."

If you are prone to lose your temper quickly or often (actually, people don't *lose* their temper, they *find* it), consider carefully what Solomon said about a quick-tempered person.

- *A quick temper is foolish:* "A quick-tempered person does foolish things, and the one who devises evil schemes is hated."[8]

- *A quick temper is divisive:* "A hot-tempered person stirs up conflict."[9]

- *A quick temper is destructive:* "A hot-tempered person must pay the penalty; rescue them, and you will have to do it again."[10]

If you consistently, constantly, and continuously lose your temper, ultimately you will be the one who loses. You will lose friends, you will lose the love of your wife, and you will lose the respect of your colleagues and your children. It may even cause you to lose your health.

John Hunter, a physiologist who had a severe heart condition, said, "My life is at the mercy of the person who can make me angry…The first scoundrel that gets me angry will kill me." People are in jails, hospitals, and morgues today because of uncontrolled anger.

You can and should control your temper. Don't blame your anger on someone or something. Solomon made this astute observation: "He who is slow to anger is better than the mighty, and he who rules his spirit than he who takes a city."[11]

Anger is like a river. A river controlled can generate enough electricity to power an entire city. But if allowed to overflow its banks, it can become a raging flood that destroys everything in its path. As surely as a river can be controlled, so can your temper. You can control your temper if you really want to, and I will prove it to you.

Have you ever been in a bitter argument in your home, either with your wife or one of your kids? I'm talking about the old-fashioned kind when everybody is yelling at the top of their lungs, going at it tooth and tong. About that time the phone rings, and instantly you pick it up and say hello in a soft, controlled tone. What happened? You just proved that you *can* tame your anger. Now learn to channel that response in your interactions with your family, friends, and coworkers.

> If you consistently, constantly,
> and continuously lose your temper,
> ultimately you will be the one who loses.

Keeping the Angry Dog on His Leash

King Solomon gave some wise old advice on how to handle this age-old problem. Let's break it down:

First, learn to slow down. "A hot-tempered person stirs up conflict, but the one who is patient calms a quarrel," Solomon says.[12] He repeatedly admonishes his children to be patient and slow to get angry (see Proverbs 14:29; 16:32; 19:11). When you are angry, count to ten before you speak. If you are real angry, count to a hundred—and then don't say anything. If you are headed toward the house of anger, be slow to arrive and walk in and extremely quick to run out the back door. The more calmly you see a situation, the more clearly you will see how to handle it.

Second, learn to judge. "Whoever is patient has great understanding," the ancient king advises, "but one who is quick-tempered displays folly."[13] Remember that not everything is worth getting angry about. When you feel your temperature rising, ask yourself, *Is this worth getting angry over?*

Similarly, teach your kids to ask two questions when they feel their anger surface: (1) Is this really worth my anger? If the answer is yes, then (2) Is this the best way, place, and time to express my anger? I know it's hard to do this in the heat of the moment, but emotions can be tamed and the temper can be trained. So learn to judge each situation accordingly.

Third, learn to respond well. "A gentle answer turns away wrath, but a harsh word stirs up anger."[14] Have you ever noticed that a fire department almost never fights fire with fire? Water is almost always a better tool. In the same way, a soft reply to an angry comment is like putting the cold water of calmness on the fire of a hot temper.

Fourth, learn to let go. "A person's wisdom yields patience; it is to one's glory to overlook an offense."[15] Never kill a fly with a sledgehammer. When you are wronged, the question is not, are you big enough to do something about it? The question is, are you big enough *not* to?

My wife and I have always tried to live by the apostle Paul's rule in Ephesians 4:26: "'In your anger do not sin': Do not let the sun go down while you are still angry." When we got married, Teresa and I agreed not to go to sleep when we are angry. To be honest, this created a few sleepless nights early in our marriage. But over time, this rule has also taught us to let our anger go.

> Anger is an acid that can do more harm to the vessel it is stored in than to anything it is poured on.

Never store the acid of anger in the container of your body. Anger is an acid that can do more harm to the vessel it is stored in than to anything it is poured on. Like milk that sours, anger that is not quickly disposed of will curdle into the cancer of bitterness that can destroy your marriage and family.

Anger is to be a servant, not a master. As Solomon says, "Fools give full vent to their rage, but the wise bring calm in the end."[16] Either you control your temper or your temper controls you. Don't allow your temper to put you on a leash; you keep it on a leash.

The importance of this virtue to fathers has been brought to my attention afresh and anew by one of God's best and latest gifts in life—grandchildren. As I type, my granddaughter is pulling on my leg hair to tell me she wants Teddy Grahams. I just finished cleaning up the aftermath of my grandson's "accident." I never once thought about fussing at either one of them for bothering me while I was working nor scolding them for "doing their business" in such an unbusinesslike manner. My patience with my grandchildren is seemingly limitless and my temper nonexistent. I am left to wonder why it couldn't have been more like that with my three precious sons and the wife I treasure so.

So, dads, learn this lesson early and easy. Don't singe your family with the flames of your anger. And begin teaching your children now to control their own. Then perhaps someday, if someone does invent a time machine, you'll find yourself heading back to relive memories rather than repair damage.

Develop the Discipline of Discipline

*"The thing that impresses me most about America,
is the way parents obey their children."*

EDWARD, DUKE OF WINDSOR

One of the most difficult acts of fathering is disciplining our children. Every parent must determine when and where to draw lines, how much is too much, how often is too frequent, and which methods to use. Take it from this father of three, you'll likely look back and question whether you made the right decisions in each case.

John Wilmot, the Earl of Rochester, once said, "Before I got married I had six theories about bringing up children. Now I have six children and no theories." As a father who has run through the parenting gauntlet, I still feel that way. But the difficulty of these decisions doesn't mean you can avoid this crucial, controversial, and consequential topic.

> Juvenile delinquency is increasing seven times faster
> than the population. Why the rapid increase?
> In part, because of delinquent parents.

It is *crucial* because we are seeing an unprecedented break-down in civility and authority in our nation, caused largely by the breakdown of authority in the home. It is *controversial* because God's Word says one thing, while many educators, sociologists, and child psychologists say another. It is *consequential* because juvenile delinquency is increasing seven times faster than the population. Why the rapid increase? In part, because of delinquent parents.

Years ago, an unknown author created a list of twelve rules on "How to Train Your Child to Be a Delinquent":

1. When your kid is still an infant, give him everything he wants. This way he will think the world owes him a living when he grows up.

2. When he picks up swearing and off-color jokes, laugh at him, encourage him. As he grows up, he will pick up cuter phrases that will floor you.

3. Never give him any spiritual training. Wait until he is twenty-one and let him decide for himself.

4. Avoid using the word *wrong*. It will give your child a guilt complex. You can condition him to believe later, when he is arrested for stealing a car, that society is against him and he is being persecuted.

5. Pick up after him—his books, shoes, and clothes. Do everything for him so he will be experienced in throwing all responsibility onto others.

6. Let him read all printed material he can get his hands on [and never think of monitoring his TV programs]. Sterilize the silverware, but let his mind feast on garbage.

7. Quarrel frequently in his presence, and then he won't be too surprised when his home is broken up later.

8. Satisfy his every craving for food, drink, and comfort. Every sensual desire must be gratified; denial may lead to harmful frustrations.

9. Give your child all the spending money he wants. Don't make him earn his own. Why should he have things as tough as you did?

10. Take his side against neighbors, teachers, and policemen. They're all against him.

11. When he gets into real trouble, make up excuses for yourself by saying, "I never could do anything with him; he's just a bad seed."

12. Prepare for a life of grief.

If you have thrown up your hands from time to time and cried out, "Help, I'm a parent!" (if you haven't gotten there yet, you will), there is hope for the hopeless and help for the helpless. The Ultimate Father has given His infinitely wise philosophy on home building and child rearing, and it can be a life preserver to many families who are sinking in a sea of conflict, quarreling, and rebellion.

I admit that the way I view this is naturally colored by the way I was reared as a child. You may have seen the timeless Smith Barney commercial where the distinguished gentleman looks into the camera and says, "They make money the old-fashioned way—they *earn* it." Well, I received my spankings as a child the old-fashioned way—I earned them! I freely (and now gratefully) admit that I was reared in a home where firm but godly discipline was practiced. My dad could clear leather quicker than Wyatt Earp!

Regardless of how you view the discipline of children, both in its necessity and in its application, the Scripture rightly says, "They sow the wind and reap the whirlwind."[1] As Leonardo da Vinci once said, "He who does not punish evil, commands it to be done."

Laying the Foundation

A newspaper article headlined "Fortress-like Dallas School Points Way" gives us a sign of the times:

> The public school of the future is open now—in Dallas. Townview Magnet Center, a $41 million state-of-the-art schoolhouse, opened this school year. With parents, politicians and school officials across the nation concerned about rising violence on school campuses, the Texas facility is likely to set the standard for new schools, particularly those in urban districts located in or near high-crime neighborhoods.
>
> It is a sprawling brick building with thirty-seven surveillance cameras, six metal detectors, five full-time police officers, and a high-tech environmental design geared toward crime prevention.
>
> That design features unusually wide halls, straight lines without nooks and crannies, lots of windows so that the school grounds can be viewed easily from inside, perimeter lights in all public spaces, and an iron pole fence that separates the school from the adjacent neighborhood.
>
> "We've decided to overdo it up front to overpower this issue," Dallas School District Superintendent Chad Woolery told the *New York Times*. "We want to make sure that safety is not an issue so kids can concentrate on learning." There is something sad about a school like Townview that is as much fortress as it is learning

institution. But, given the realities of life in so many of our public schools today, it is hard to argue against it.[2]

What does all of this have to do with the discipline of children in the home? Simply everything. Former Commissioner of Education Ernest L. Boyer correctly sized up the situation when he said,

> The schools are a reflection of the world around them. Schools don't operate in a vacuum. You show me a school that has discipline and high standards, and I'll find you homes in a community that operate along those value systems. A school that has become chaotic, and where there is a lack of respect and commitment to work hard, probably reflects behavior that occurs once children leave the school.[3]

> The foundation of our society is cracking, in part, because the foundations of our homes are crumbling.

This is a sad testament to the failure of many parents to lovingly but firmly discipline their children. Our homes affect our schools. Our schools affect our communities. And our communities shape our society. The foundation of our society is cracking, in part, because the foundations of our homes are crumbling.

Timing Is Everything

A pithy little proverb nestled right in the middle of Solomon's book summarizes his counsel on this matter of rearing children:

> Train up a child in the way he should go,
> And when he is old he will not depart from it.[4]

Whether or not you have heard that verse before, you may find yourself muttering under your breath, "Is that it?" But before you dismiss this short statement as simplistic, consider that it contains an ocean of profound truth able, if properly understood and applied, to make a world of difference in you as a parent and in your children.

In the 1992 presidential campaign, Bill Clinton's manager, James Carville, encapsulated the driving concern of the election with four simple words: "It's the economy, stupid!" When it comes to the discipline, training, and rearing of your children, "It's the timing, dads!"

The subject of Proverbs 22:6 is a child. The word translated "train up" can be translated "dedicate." In other words, it is from childbirth that we are to dedicate our children to the Lord, and the instruction of discipline is to start when children are young. There may be a dad reading this chapter who needs to stop worrying about what Junior will do when he grows up, put this book down, and go see what he's up to *now*!

Solomon is not advising us on how to train up a teenager or a young man; his advice is on how to "train up a *child*." There are two reasons why it is important to start early in the training and disciplining of children.

First, the will is more flexible. A twig is much easier to bend than a trunk. The time to train a child in the ways of life and to teach a child the things of God is when that child is young. In the early years, the child's will is like soft clay, malleable and pliable. It is when they are young that you are to "set their ways," for when they get older their "ways are set."

The Hebrew verb "train up" came from agrarian terminology and referred to training a tree or vine to grow in a particular shape or direction.[5] If you have ever been to Disney World, you have seen those fascinating shrubs shaped like animals and various Disney characters. Recently, I had the privilege of doing a

"Backstage Tour" of Disney World, and I witnessed how those bushes are formed.

From the time the bushes are planted until they are ten to fifteen years old, they are shaped, trimmed, pruned, and trained in the way that they should go. Some parts are removed, other parts are cultivated, and still other parts are trimmed away. Finally, the entire plant conforms to a wire mesh in the shape of the desired animal or character.

That process is similar to the way we are to train our children. It must begin early, for as Solomon reminds us: "Discipline your children while there is hope. Otherwise you will ruin their lives."[6] I can't tell you how many times parents in my church have come to my office, brokenhearted over their children, and told me, "My kids are hopeless." Usually the reason their kids are hopeless is that the parents didn't train their children while there was still hope.

You can almost hear the urgency in Solomon's voice as he said, "A refusal to correct is a refusal to love; love your children by disciplining them."[7] Other translations of this verse indicate that the discipline should be carried out "promptly" or "diligently." Dad, the two greatest words of advice I can give you on rearing your children are *start early*.

You may have a little darling running around your house right now who you think is a little angel. But trust me, one day those legs will get longer, those wings will get shorter, and sometimes those little angels even sprout horns!

You don't have to be a rocket scientist to figure out that it's far easier to talk to and reason with a child in his younger years than when he becomes a teenager. When they are young, they are more apt and ready to listen to your advice and counsel. Children are hungry to learn, and they haven't yet reached the age where they think they know everything and you know nothing.

> Teach your kids while they are young and will still
> listen to you. The day will come when they won't.

Mark Twain said that when he was fourteen years old, he thought his father was the dumbest man in the world. By the time he reached twenty-one, he was amazed how much his dad had learned in seven years. The famous author felt like many adolescents do, so teach your kids while they are young and will still listen to you. The day will come when they won't.

While they are in the "listening stage," you should be in the "talking and teaching stage." Take your children on walks and share wise words with them. And make sure you take the opportunity to read the Bible to your children. Use everyday experiences to teach them what God's Word has to say about how to treat others, how to be polite, how to forgive, and how to love fellow human beings. Never underestimate God's truths to your children even at an early age.

The *second* reason to start early is because when children are young, *the heart is more tender.* Your children are more impressionable early on. Love them, shepherd them, and shape them while their heart is still soft.

Get Back to the Basics

As I scoured God's letter to dads in the book of Proverbs, I discovered four basic principles to guide fathers as they make decisions about disciplining their children. Following these principles will help you become the best parent you can be in this area.

1. The Principle of Affection

Solomon says, "A refusal to correct is a refusal to love; love your children by disciplining them."[8] Many parents are afraid that discipline will drive their child from them, but the ancient king says the opposite is true. Rather than causing your child to question your love, discipline applied in the right way at the right time affirms and confirms your love. Love and discipline go together. If you love your children, you will discipline them, but you will discipline them *in love*. I cannot overemphasize the importance of a child knowing and feeling real affection from their dad.

> Love and discipline go together.
> If you love your children, you will discipline them,
> but you will discipline them *in love*.

I recently read the tragic comments of a former US Open champion golfer, Hubert Green. His recounting of his relationship with both his father and subsequently his children is sad and sobering:

> I never really knew my dad. I never saw my mom and him kiss or hug, and he never hugged us. Not once. He never praised us. I worked so hard to get his approval but it never came. One year I took him to Japan. I played well and decided to spring for first-class tickets on the way home. We were somewhere over the Pacific when Dad, with a bourbon and water in his hand, turned to me and said, "Son, you done good." For the next five hours, I was higher than the plane.
>
> I'm sure my upbringing had something to do with me not being a great father myself. I felt awkward trying to show affection to my three boys, counseling them and everything else I was supposed to do. Finally I said, "I'm trying to give you the love you need, trying

to show you the way, and I'm doing a poor job because I don't know how. I'm asking you to forgive me, and for your help. I need help helping you." I'd like to say my speech cured everything, but it didn't. I envy these fathers who say how much fun parenting is, because for me it was work. I never did get good at it.[9]

I do not buy the age-old excuse that parents don't discipline their children because they "love them too much." The truth is, if you don't discipline your children, it's because you love *yourself* too much. A Gallup poll revealed that more than 90 percent of graduating high school seniors wished their parents and teachers loved them enough to discipline them more and require more of them.[10]

Solomon had a method in his madness when he wrote,

> My son, do not despise the LORD's discipline,
>   and do not resent his rebuke,
> because the LORD disciplines those he loves,
>   as a father the son he delights in.[11]

Any parents who refuse to discipline their children are really saying they are better parents than God.

The greatest and wisest father of all is God. God not only loves, God *is* love. Yet we read here that a loving God is a God who disciplines. So try this on for an earth-shattering thought: Any parents who refuse to discipline their children are really saying they are better parents than God.

Remember, love always does what is best for the other person. Discipline is painful, often distasteful, and sometimes downright depressing, but love demands and commands discipline and training for the child.

2. The Principle of Direction

"A youngster's heart is filled with foolishness," Solomon said, "but physical discipline will drive it far away."[12] He's not telling us to beat our children; rather, he's teaching us that we must actively direct our children in the best path for their lives. His concern is with foolishness, not childishness. You are not to discipline a child just because they act like a child. How else can they act? You should not discipline a child because he makes childish mistakes, such as knocking his milk over or (even more infuriating) laughing at his sister when she knocks hers over.

Folly may sound mischievous to us, but for the ancient Hebrew it was a far more serious matter. In Proverbs, the opposite of folly is wisdom, and the lack of wisdom results in wickedness. Folly here equates to wickedness. Folly is the spirit of rebellion that despises discipline and disrespects authority.

The natural tendency of any child is to rebel (this has been true since the Garden of Eden). This tendency must be driven from the child. Just as a car, out of line, tends to drift and needs constant correction, every child is born spiritually out of line and needs to be constantly corrected by his parents.

Solomon went on to observe, "To discipline a child produces wisdom, but a mother is disgraced by an undisciplined child."[13] Now, why is this true? It's true because a child left to himself is a child left in the condition in which he was born. He was born out of line. He was born in folly. The child must, therefore, learn moral authority. He must learn that for every action there is a reaction.

Dad, remember that you are a tool in the hands of God to direct your children from where they *would* go to where they *should* go. This is the purpose as well as the necessity of godly discipline.

> Too many parents make the mistake of always
> telling their children when they are wrong, rather
> than also taking the time to tell them how to
> get right, be right, and stay right.

3. The Principle of Correction

Too many parents make the mistake of always telling their children when they are wrong, rather than also taking the time to tell them how to get right, be right, and stay right. Biblical correction involves both. The number one extrabiblical beatitude for all parents is, "Blessed are the balanced."

Solomon went on to write, "Discipline your children, and they will give you peace; they will bring you the delights you desire."[14] The word *discipline* means to correct, to reprove, or to force back to the right way. Always remember that discipline is like a two-edged sword; it is not only to correct children when they are wrong, but to direct them to a way that is right.

During my middle son's senior year of high school, I had to make a very difficult decision that affected him directly. He was infuriated by my choice, and ended up giving me the silent treatment for three months. He literally did not speak one word to me for ninety days. If I addressed him, he returned my words with a cold stare. I could beg and even send in his mother (who he has always listened to more than me), but nothing made a difference.

At the time, I thought I was burning a bridge with Jonathan, but I felt so strongly about the decision, I stuck by it. After three months, he ended up talking to me but just barely. A year later, we were speaking civilly but not warmly. By the time he graduated from college, we had begun to relate to each other again as father and son. Today, we are the best of friends. Was the price I paid worth it? I can't say with any degree of certainty. But even my son will tell you that, looking back, he respects that I tried to make a decision out of love and concern for him.

Dad, you may as well quit trying to win a popularity contest with your children. You will lose—to teammates, classmates, and girlfriends and boyfriends. Your children are not always going to like you. But if you will discipline them, correct them, keep them from going the wrong way, and continually lead them back to the right way, they will love you—and eventually they will grow to like you again if they ever truly stopped.

4. The Principle of Protection

As dads, we don't often think of discipline as a form of protection, perhaps because it hurts both parties so much. But Solomon actually links the two:

> Don't fail to discipline your children.
>   They won't die if you spank them.
> Physical discipline
>   may well save them from death.[15]

> Discipline, or the lack thereof, can set off a positive or a negative chain reaction in the life of your child.

Now we begin to see what is at stake in the matter of discipline. Solomon says that the protection of your children—indeed, their very soul—is at risk. Discipline, or the lack thereof, can set off a positive or a negative chain reaction in the life of your child. If a child will not respect authority in the home, he will not respect it in the school, the government, the church, or, ultimately, even heaven itself. It is just a small step from rebelling against the parents that God gave a child to rebelling against the God who gave the child his parents.

Four Rules for Effective Discipline

As I have said, I wasn't always the perfect disciplinarian. Looking back, I was probably too harsh. I wish I hadn't let a bad day or a stressful season push me over the edge and prompt me to make snap decisions. I should have been more graceful than I was at times. If I were to start the parenting process again today, here are four rules I'd live by:

1. Start disciplining earlier, not later.

When a child is old enough to disobey willingly and knowingly, when a child is old enough to know right from wrong and chooses wrong over right, when a child is old enough to be told to do what is right and then does what is wrong anyway—that child is ready to be guided.

Your kids will reach an age where certain types of discipline are inappropriate. So use discernment here and get lots of wise counsel from those who have gone before you. You will give an account to God for the authority that you exercised over your children.

2. Make sure guidelines are clear.

Child psychologists discovered an interesting truth several years ago. Contemporary thought assumed that fences on playgrounds made children feel restricted in their recreation. Based on that belief, it was decided to remove the fences so children would not feel confined. To the astonishment of the experts, the opposite effect occurred. Children became more inhibited with their activities. They tended to huddle toward the middle of the playground and exhibited signs of insecurity. When the fences were replaced, the children once more played with greater enthusiasm and freedom.

We all need boundaries—something to define the limits of safety and security. The experts suggested that boundaries restrict creativity, but as the children on the playground demonstrated, they needed a clear understanding of what is safe and acceptable so their creativity could flourish. Children will flourish, and you will function better as a dad, if guidelines are clearly communicated and the consequence of not following those guidelines completely understood.

Before I gave my first son the keys to his first car, he signed a contract that I drew up. We went over every item of that contract, and then we both signed it. Here is the contract we signed:

Contract with Character for a Car

- I agree to pay for all the gas.
- Any speeding violations will result in loss of driving privileges of up to one month, depending on the severity of the violation.
- I understand there will be a graduated schedule of where I can travel, which will increase with experience, age, and demonstrated maturity.
- If I incur any accidents that are my fault, I will lose one month of driving privileges.
- Only passengers approved by both sets of parents may be transported, and for the first year, only one passenger at a time without special permission from Mom and Dad.
- Reckless driving will incur loss of driving privileges of up to one month.
- Earning less than satisfactory grades in school will result in the loss of driving privileges of one month.
- No parking in secluded spots with a member of the opposite sex *under any circumstances.*
- On school nights, I will be allowed one night a week

out but must adhere to my curfew unless special permission is granted (exceptions to curfews granted per individual case/circumstances).

- Whereabouts must be given to Mom and Dad at all times within reason.

- Chores must be done at home as part of maintaining driving privileges.

- Attitude, obedience, responsibility, and conduct may determine availability of car.

- I may take either brother only when prior permission is granted or in case of an emergency.

I, the undersigned, understand and agree to adhere to all the above conditions and fix my signature hereto.

Signature: _____(Driver)

Signature: _____(Parents)

Before he ever turned the ignition switch, my son clearly understood the guidelines under which he could keep the privilege of driving the car. Looking back, I wish I'd been this clear and explicit with other areas of my children's lives. If they don't know the rules, they cannot follow them. And when they break rules they weren't aware of, you both wind up losing.

3. Render discipline appropriately.

Solomon refers frequently to the "rod of discipline" or to "physical discipline," depending on which translation you use.[16] Solomon was advocating neither child abuse nor literal beatings. What he teaches us by the use of that imagery is that we are to discipline appropriately. At times that may include physical discipline, but we should never use physical discipline as a weapon we unleash to help us blow off steam.

If you choose to spank your child (and I'm not opposed to spanking if it is done appropriately), use extreme caution because it is the discipline method where you can most easily make destructive mistakes. Do not spank your child frequently. Spankings need to be few and far between. Do not spank your child angrily. Never—I repeat, never—strike your child in anger. Never spank your child with your hand. No child should ever be hit with a hand, open or closed. That's not discipline; that's abuse, and the Bible condemns it. And, finally, if you have a short or strong temper, you may need to forego all corporal punishment for other forms of discipline. I can tell you from my own experience that even one spanking given in raw anger can scar your child and leave you with lifelong regrets. Godly punishment is always administered in love and with tender affirmation afterward.

4. Administer discipline privately.

The purpose of discipline is instruction not humiliation. You should never embarrass a child in public. I remember an instance when one of my children was talking in church while I was preaching. I stopped preaching and called him out in front of the entire congregation. This was wrong, and later in life I apologized to him for my mistake.

Helping the Child to Sit Down and the Adult to Stand Up

Returning to Proverbs 22:6 for a moment, we uncover a profound truth in the verb "train up." In Hebrew, that word roots back to a term referring to the palate or the roof of the mouth. In ancient days, a Hebrew mother would wean her baby off milk by taking her index finger and dipping it into some crushed grapes or dates. She would then place that finger into the mouth of the child and massage the gums and the palate, creating a sucking response. This would soon cultivate a desire for more food. In this way the child was taught to crave, and then swallow, solid food.

> The best way to get your children to accept the truth is not just to teach it but to live it.

Solomon is giving us here a gentle reminder that we are not to ram truth down the throats of our children, but we are to make them hungry for it so they will freely swallow and digest it. It should go without saying, dad, that the best way to get your children to accept the truth is not just to teach it but to live it.

We are then told to train up children "in the way they should go." The word *way* is extremely picturesque. It refers to the bending of a bow. Literally it says, "Train up a child in his way." That is, train up a child in the way he is bent. Bible scholar Walter Kaiser explained the concept perfectly:

> What is the "way"? It could mean the way that the child ought to go according to God's law: the proper way in light of God's revelation. It could also mean the way best fitting the child's own personality and particular traits.
>
> Which is correct? There is no doubt that the first presents the highest standard and more traditional meaning. However, it has the least support from the Hebrew idiom and seems to be a cryptic way to state what other proverbial expressions would have done much more explicitly.
>
> Therefore, we conclude that this enigmatic phrase means that instruction ought to be conformed to the nature of the youth. It ought to regulate itself according to the stage of life, evidence of God's unique

calling of the child, and the manner of life for which God is singling out that child.[17]

Every child is to be trained in the way of the Lord, but in the words of Derek Kidner, in "respect for his individuality and vocation, though not for his selfwill."[18] The *Amplified Bible* captures the sense perfectly: "Train up a child in the way he should go [and *in keeping with his individual gift or bent]*, and when he is old he will not depart from it" (italics added).

This cornerstone verse refers not only to the *material* of instruction (the wisdom found in God's Word) but also to the *manner* of instruction that is to be governed by the child's unique stage of life, personality, and giftedness—his personal bent.

> Don't try to live your life through your children. You should train up children in the way *they should* go, not the way *you would* go.

Your children are just like my three sons in one way: each one is different from the others. I have had to learn that I cannot treat every child exactly the same. Of course, certain principles apply to all our children, but you cannot always treat children in the same way for the simple reason that all children are not the same. Therefore, avoid these two mistakes at all costs:

First, don't try to make your children into what you used to be. Just because you were a football player doesn't mean your son will want to be one. Just because you made straight As in school doesn't mean your daughter is capable of a 4.0 grade-point average. I'm not trying to excuse laziness, but children are not equally gifted athletically or intellectually.

Second, don't try to make your children into what you wanted to be. Don't try to live your life through your children. Just because you didn't fulfill your dream to become a doctor doesn't mean you should try to force your child to become one. The verse says to train up children in the way *they should* go, not the way *you would* go.

Dads must teach their kids to *know* who they are, to *like* who they are, and to *be* who they are. Indeed, those are the three marks of healthy self-esteem.

Some Apples Fall Farther from the Tree

Solomon says if we train up our children, when they are old, "they will not depart from it." A great illustration of this comes from two families—one named Edwards, the other named Jukes. They started out with differing philosophies and ended up with differing legacies, and the difference was discipline.

> The father of Jonathan Edwards was a minister. His mother was the daughter of a clergyman. Among their descendants were fourteen presidents of colleges, more than one hundred college professors, more than one hundred lawyers, thirty judges, sixty physicians, more than a hundred clergymen, missionaries, and theology professors, and about sixty authors. There is scarcely any great American industry that has not had one of his family among its chief promoters. Such is the product of one American Christian family, reared under the most favorable conditions.
>
> The contrast is presented in the Jukes family, which could not be made to study, would not work, and is said to have cost the State of New York a million dollars. Their entire record is one of pauperism and crime, insanity, and imbecility. Among their twelve hundred known descendants, three hundred and ten were

professional paupers, four hundred and forty were physically wrecked by their own wickedness, sixty were habitual thieves, one hundred and thirty were convicted criminals, fifty-five were victims of impurity. Only twenty learned a trade (and ten of these learned in the state prison), and this notorious family produced seven murderers.[19]

Yes, discipline does make a difference! Kids in the Edwards family were disciplined, and when they grew old, they bore the fruit of their parents' investments. If children are reared by godly principles, they can multiply the influence of an entire family for generations to come.

But keep in mind proverbs are not so much promises as they are principles and precepts.[20] You might be a dad who lives under a cloud of guilt because you have a prodigal child, and you wonder if you are a father-failure. But sometimes a child simply will not listen to the counsel of his parents. I'm sure Solomon was giving a word of personal testimony when he wrote, "A wise son heeds his father's instruction, but a mocker does not respond to rebukes."[21] Bad parents sometimes turn out good children, and good parents sometimes have bad children. Remember, God's first two children were put in a perfect paradise...and they rebelled anyway.

From all this I conclude that if you begin disciplining early and continue right up through adolescence, the teenage years, and beyond—if you train those children in godly principles according to their unique nature, setting a godly example before them—then, generally speaking, they will not depart from it. Proper discipline is the best bet you have for directing your child into their best future.

Dads have a tough job, no doubt about it, but let us covenant together to stay the course and be true fathers. This means lovingly and carefully disciplining our children. It's not a foolproof plan, but it is a good one. With the help of God's power, the wisdom of His Word, and the leadership of His Spirit, we help our children enter into the adult world ready to make it a better world for all of us.

6

Don't Be Afraid of Birds or Bees

"The monstrosity of sexual intercourse outside marriage is that those who indulge in it are trying to isolate one kind of union from all the other kinds of union which were intended to go along with it and make up the total union."

C.S. LEWIS, *MERE CHRISTIANITY*

I remember when I had the "sex talk" with my eldest son. It was more a process of asking him if he had any questions than a full-on course in human sexuality. When it concluded, I walked out of the room with a shiny forehead and sweat rings under my arms. Collapsing onto my bed, I thought to myself, *I probably should have prepared a bit more for that.*

Having this infamous conversation with our kids is never easy. Parents are mortified by it, and so are our children. Maybe that's why we often have it too late. According to a recent study published in *Pediatrics*, researchers found that more than 40 percent of adolescents had experienced sexual intercourse before they had talked with their parents about sex. What makes that statistic especially troubling is that the study also found that teens who do talk to their parents about sex are more likely to delay their first sexual encounter.[1]

Of course, some parents at least attempt to broach this

sensitive subject early in life. But when they do, they are unpre-
pared and end up speaking in obscure generalities. This type of
conversation isn't of much help to either party.

"A lot of parents think they had a conversation, and the kids
don't remember it at all," says Karen Soren, director of adolescent
medicine at New York-Presbyterian Morgan Stanley Children's
Hospital. "Parents sometimes say things more vaguely because
they are uncomfortable and they think they've addressed something, but the kids don't hear the topic at all."[2]

> Having the infamous sex talk with our kids
> is never easy. Parents are mortified by it,
> and so are our children.

When it comes to almost any subject our kids want to discuss,
we dads can wing it without any problem. Sports? We can tell
them how we almost won the Heisman Trophy—in high school.
Cars? We can regale them with tales of the first car we ever owned
that we bought with our own money or built with our own hands.
We can even discuss God without much of a problem; many dads
wax eloquent in the role of "The Right Reverend Father."

But when we try to bring up the subject of sex, we have a very
difficult time. Our hearts palpitate, palms sweat, faces twitch,
and voices crack. After giving our children a stumbling mess of
words, we conclude with the only response we can muster: "Go
ask your mother." Surely, this topic deserves a better effort than
we often give it.

Many of us face a twofold problem over this sensitive but critically important topic. On the one hand, fathers are not talking or
are waiting too late to talk, while children are not asking because
they are getting their information somewhere else. I think of the

dad who nervously sat down with his fourth-grade son and said, "Tommy, don't you think it's time we had a talk about sex?" Little Tommy responded, "Sure, Dad, what do you want to know?"

> The sad fact is, our children are getting their sex education in schools, the theater, television, magazines, billboards, and computers, but not at home.

The sad fact is, our children are getting their sex education in schools, the theater, television, magazines, billboards, and computers, but not at home. Solomon wisely observed about the person who goes wrong in the area of sex: "He shall die for lack of instruction, and in the greatness of his folly he shall go astray."[3]

Did you notice how he lamented the lack of proper instruction? Today, our children suffer physically from venereal disease, emotionally from guilt, and spiritually from sexual sin—and much of it is because they are not being taught in the right classroom by the right teacher.

For too long, both pastors and fathers have kept their heads in the sand, hoping this topic would just go away. But the subject cannot be avoided. Pollster George Gallup once stated, "There's no question about it, the sex-related issues are going to be the most important issues facing all churches in the foreseeable future. Abortion, AIDS, pre-marital sex, homosexuality—all those are going to be at the vortex."[4] Gallup said that almost two decades ago—a true prophet!

But there is another problem still: education alone, especially school-based sex education, is not a panacea for all our sexual problems. We cannot educate our children in a moral vacuum. Instead, we must work hard to instill in them the virtues of a life well lived. Sex education *is* the answer as long as it involves the right teacher, the right classroom, and the right curriculum. The right teacher is you, dad. The right classroom is your home. And the right curriculum is the Bible.

> Our children need fathers who will shoot straight about sex. Studies show that parental involvement is the single most critical factor affecting the sexual activity of teens.

Our children need fathers who will shoot straight about sex. Studies show that parental involvement is the single most critical factor affecting the sexual activity of teens. A study of ten thousand high-school sophomores, conducted by the US Department of Education, found that strong parental values and parental supervision have the most significant effect on teens' sexual activity. Parents who had a close relationship with their teenage daughter and supervised her schoolwork and activities were able to curb by 42 percent the likelihood that their daughter would become pregnant.[5]

Solomon got involved early and strongly in educating kids about God's perspective on sex. The three largest sections in Proverbs dealing with a single topic are found in chapters 5 through 7. In chapters 5 and 6, Solomon dealt extensively with premarital sex. He devoted almost the entirety of chapter 7 to extramarital sex. In between, he gave a frank discussion of sex within the will of God. Let's take a look at what God wants every dad to know about this nerve-racking topic.

Danger Ahead

Drawing from both divine wisdom and human experience, Solomon vividly described the factors that lead one to sexual catastrophe: a person who is susceptible, another immoral person who is available, and illicit sex that is desirable. When that combination appears, bad things are not only possible, they're probable. The spiral to sexual sin happens in three steps.

Step 1: Sexual sin begins with foolish exposure.

> I saw among the simple,
>> I noticed among the young men,
>> a youth who had no sense.
> He was going down the street near her corner,
>> walking along in the direction of her house
> at twilight, as the day was fading,
>> as the dark of night set in.[6]

The susceptible person is in the wrong place at the wrong time with the wrong person. This is always a recipe for disaster. The first lesson to teach our children about sex is this: If you don't want to get burned, stay out of the kitchen. You cannot get hooked on cocaine if you never use it. You cannot become an alcoholic if you never drink it. You cannot commit sexual sin if you do not allow yourself to get into the wrong situation.

I heard about one elderly gentleman who noticed a little boy going around and around the block on his tricycle. This went on for about two hours. Finally the old man stopped the boy and said, "Son, aren't you getting tired? You've been going around this block all morning."

"I'm running away from home," the little boy said.

"But you're not running away from home. You're just going around the block."

"No, I am running away from home, but my mommy said I couldn't cross the street."

The fact is, we are all prone to wander. But God has laid down the law and set certain boundaries we should not cross, certain places we should not go, and certain people we should never accompany. There is never a right time to be in the wrong place with the wrong person.

What a lot of parents call trust, I call neglect. Psychologist Henry Brandt tells how his son got upset with him when Brandt would not permit him to go down to the lake in a car alone with a girl after dark. "What's wrong, Dad?" the son said. "Don't you trust me?"

"In a car, alone at night, in front of a lake, with a beautiful girl?" Brandt asked. "I wouldn't trust me. Why should I trust you?"[7]

Step 2: Sexual sin continues with flirtatious excitement.

> She took hold of him and kissed him
> > and with a brazen face she said:
> "Today I fulfilled my vows,
> > and I have food from my fellowship offering at home.
> So I came out to meet you;
> > I looked for you and have found you!
> I have covered my bed
> > with colored linens from Egypt.
> I have perfumed my bed
> > with myrrh, aloes and cinnamon.
> Come, let's drink deeply of love till morning;
> > let's enjoy ourselves with love!"[8]

This picture is three thousand years old, but it can quickly be brought up-to-date. The bed could be a king-sized Tempur-Pedic or the backseat of a car. The linens could be thick carpet in front of a fireplace. The spices could be beer, pizza, and soft music playing in the background. Notice how this woman used the young man's eyes and ears as a pipeline to his heart. Flattery was the bait and her tongue was the hook. Solomon often referred to the sexual dangers of flattery:

To deliver you from the immoral woman,
From the seductress who flatters with her words.[9]

For the lips of the adulterous woman drip honey,
    and her speech is smoother than oil.[10]

For this command is a lamp,
    this teaching is a light,
and correction and instruction
    are the way to life,
keeping you from your neighbor's wife,
    from the smooth talk of a wayward woman.[11]

They will keep you from the adulterous woman,
    from the wayward woman with her seductive
      words.[12]

With persuasive words she led him astray;
    she seduced him with her smooth talk.[13]

> Sweet talk can lead to a sour experience, which can poison a life. Flattery should trigger the alarm, "Danger ahead!"

Just because Solomon is speaking about a seductive woman doesn't mean his warning can't apply to men as well. Dad, your daughters need to be on guard against silver-tongued boys. Sweet talk can lead to a sour experience, which can poison a life. Flattery should trigger the alarm, "Danger ahead!"

Step 3: Sexual sin leads to a fatal experience.

Listen to the way Eugene Peterson translates these verses about the seductive, adulterous woman:

Soon she has him eating out of her hand,
    bewitched by her honeyed speech.

Before you know it, he's trotting behind her,
   like a calf led to the butcher shop,
Like a stag lured into ambush
   and then shot with an arrow,
Like a bird flying into a net
   not knowing that its flying life is over.[14]

The lips of a seductive woman are oh so sweet,
   her soft words are oh so smooth.
But it won't be long before she's gravel in your mouth,
   a pain in your gut, a wound in your heart.
She's dancing down the primrose path to Death;
   she's headed straight for Hell and taking you with
      her.[15]

Regardless of who you are, there is a payday for sexual sin. It comes back to destroy our lives. People talk, husbands hear, pregnancies occur, diseases spread, and guilt festers. No one is immune.

Growing up, I gave my kids three rules every time they went out on a date:

1. Keep every button buttoned.

2. Keep every zipper zipped.

3. Keep every piece of clothing on.

This is frank talk, but it is the kind of talk our kids need when they enter the dating world.

Sex Leaves Scars

Solomon made it plain to his kids that they might have champagne today, but real pain would come tomorrow. Using the canvas of Scripture, he painted one of the most powerful pictures of the destructive power of sexual promiscuity to be found anywhere. Again, listen to Peterson's rendition:

> Can you build a fire in your lap
>   and not burn your pants?
> Can you walk barefoot on hot coals
>   and not get blisters?
> It's the same when you have sex with your neighbor's
>   wife:
> Touch her and you'll pay for it. No excuses.[16]

Solomon tells us sexual sin leaves several types of scars:

The scar of emotional distress. I find it interesting that Solomon compares sexual sin to being burned with fire. Doctors tell us that burns cause the most horrible scars the human body can suffer. They are the most obvious, the most painful, and the most resistant to corrective surgery. When you engage someone sexually, it touches your very soul. It creates ripples into your mind and your psyche. And when you tear away from this person due to a breakup, it will damage your emotions.

The scar of physical disease. Solomon said in Proverbs 5:11, "At the end of your life you will groan, when your flesh and body are spent." You should not be surprised to learn the following:

- One out of every five Americans is now infected with a viral sexually-transmitted disease (STD)—that's fifty-six million people.

- There are nineteen million new sexually transmitted infections every year—half to those between the ages of fifteen and twenty-four.[17]

- Thirty-three thousand people a day contract a venereal disease, including six thousand teenagers.

- Twenty years ago there were four types of STDs among teenagers; today there are more than thirty.

- At the present rate, one in four Americans between the ages of fifteen and fifty-five eventually will acquire an STD.[18]

In a powerful editorial supporting sexual fidelity, the *Journal of the American Medical Association* called for an end to sexual permissiveness to stop the spread of AIDS. The *Journal* (the largest-circulating journal in the world) criticized the sexual mores of our time. The editors concluded, this is a great time to practice sexual monogamy.[19]

The scar of moral disgrace. The adulterous person will wind up saying, "I have come to the brink of utter ruin, and now I must face public disgrace."[20] Fornication and adultery are natural-born killers. They not only kill the body; they kill reputations, testimonies, spiritual vitality, clear consciences, and marriages.

The scar of spiritual defeat. God can forgive sexual sin, but study the life of King David and you will find that following his adultery with Bathsheba, he was never restored to his former power or position. The tree of promiscuity always bears bitter fruit. Though the wound heals, the scar always remains.

I need to stop right here and say a word to all of us dads. We cannot expect our kids to stay pure and control their sexual desire if we don't. I have placed in the flyleaf of my Bible a warning to men who are even thinking of straying; it's a reminder of what may happen if we do:

- Your mate will experience the anguish of betrayal, shame, rejection, heartache, and loneliness. No amount of repentance will soften those blows.

- Your mate can never again say that you are a model of fidelity. Suspicion will rob her or him of trust.

- Your escapade(s) will introduce to your life and your mate's life the very real probability of a sexually transmitted disease.

- The total devastation your sinful actions will bring to your children is immeasurable. Their growth, innocence, trust, and healthy outlook on life will be severely and permanently damaged.

- The heartache you will cause your parents, your families, and your peers is indescribable.

- Your fall will give others license to do the same.

- The inner peace you enjoyed will be wrecked.

- The name of Jesus Christ, whom you once honored, will be tarnished, giving the enemies of faith further reason to sneer and jeer at him.[21]

Dad, the price of sexual sin is too high and the cost is too great. It is a bad bargain to trade the birthright of a clear conscience for the pottage of temporary sexual excitement.

Sex Can Be Great

Remember that Solomon said sex is like a fire. That means it can be either powerfully constructive or powerfully destructive. Fire can heat your house when it is controlled or burn it to the ground if uncontrolled. And the best thing to put on a fire to keep it under control is water. That's exactly what Solomon suggested:

> Drink water from your own cistern,
>   running water from your own well.
> Should your springs overflow in the streets,
>   your streams of water in the public squares?
> Let them be yours alone,
>   never to be shared with strangers.

> May your fountain be blessed,
>> and may you rejoice in the wife of your youth.
> A loving doe, a graceful deer—
>> may her breasts satisfy you always,
>> may you ever be intoxicated with her love.[22]

Do you see how Solomon spoke of marital sex? He used the metaphors of water, cistern, well, fountain, and streams. When you understand his culture, you see why these images came to his mind.

In the ancient Near East, to have your own spring, well, or cistern was considered as valuable as gold. Clean water was a precious commodity. What Solomon was saying to his children is this: Why drink from the polluted water that comes from the sewer of promiscuous sex when, if you wait, you can drink the clean water that comes from the well of a devoted spouse?

> There is nothing as beautiful as sex with the right person, at the right place, at the right time, in the will of God.

There is nothing as beautiful as sex with the right person, at the right place, at the right time, in the will of God. A story I heard years ago says it best, and I wish every parent would tell it to their sons and daughters, particularly as they begin to enter the years of courtship and marriage.

A girl living fast and loose was trying to entice one of her friends, who was sexually pure, to join her in a jet-set lifestyle. The pure girl said to her friend, "Any time I want to become like you, I can. But you can never again become like I am."

So don't be afraid of the birds or the bees. They can't harm you, but ignoring them can bring great harm to your children.

Dad, let's teach our children and our teenagers that their bodies belong first to God. Let's teach them to fight for a life of purity as an act of worship to a good God who values sex. And let's model for them what a pure life looks like. If we can do these things, we'll help them enjoy God's beautiful gift of sex the way He has planned it from the beginning.

Work Is Important...But It's Not Everything

"I know you've heard it a thousand times before. But it's true—hard work pays off. If you want to be good, you have to practice, practice, practice. If you don't love something, then don't do it."

RAY BRADBURY, AUTHOR

When my children were young, we began giving them a meager allowance. This was done not to fund them but to mature them. They had to do chores in order to earn this. No work, no allowance. And when they received the allowance in exchange for completing their chores, they were instructed to divvy it up properly.

Each son had three jars in his room marked "tithe," "savings," and "spending." Ten percent of money earned went into the tithe jar, so they could learn the joy of giving for the benefit of others. Ten percent went into the savings jar, so they would learn the value of storing up for the future. The rest of the money was placed in the spending jar to use at their discretion. In addition to teaching them about money management, this plan instilled in them a principle too often forgotten: An honest day's wage should be exchanged for an honest day's work.

When my sons were old enough to drive, the principle was extended. We would provide them with a modest car, but they would have to pay to run and maintain it, which meant getting a job. My wife and I were clear that we would not be their personal ATMs.

Once they graduated from college, we told them they were on their own. We were not going to pay off their student loans or foot the bill for them to sit around the house and play video games instead of looking for a job. Wages can only be exchanged for work.

This is the way our home functioned, but it is also the way the world works. One of the most important principles you can instill in your children is a proper work ethic.

> We should be concerned about our children's work ethic since they will spend one-half the waking hours of their prime adult life working.

The era in which Solomon reigned functioned similarly to our own, which is why he seems fixated on the idea of laziness, returning to it repeatedly in Proverbs. We too should be concerned about our children's work ethic since they will spend one-half the waking hours of their prime adult life working.

Contrary to some thinking, *work* is not a dirty word. I have even heard some Bible teachers and preachers misinterpret work as a curse that came as a result of the Fall of Adam and Eve. Nothing could be further from the truth.

This world is the result of God's work.[1] God gave Adam the job of tending the Garden of Eden before sin came on the scene.[2] God's own Son was a carpenter.[3] Paul was a tentmaker.[4] There is nothing dishonorable about work worth doing and work done well.

President Theodore Roosevelt was right when he said, "Extend pity to no man because he has to work. If he is worth his salt, he will work. I envy the man who has work worth doing, and does it well...far and away the best prize that life offers is the chance to work hard at work worth doing."

Somehow we have lost the spirit of President Roosevelt's thinking. Ask any employer, and he will tell you that to find someone who will work hard, do the job right, and finish the task is as rare as public prayer in a public school (that's another topic for another discussion).

Dad, I believe one of the best things you can do for both the character and the reputation of your children is to pass on to them a strong work ethic and to warn them of the dangers of laziness.

It's Not That He's Lazy—He Just Won't Work

At all costs, Solomon did not want his children to become *sluggards* (a word seldom used today that describes a lifestyle very much in vogue). The wise king uses some variation of *sluggard* or *lazy* close to twenty times in Proverbs. Understand that the sluggard is not a person who would work but just cannot; the sluggard, rather, is a person who could work but will not.

As I've perused Proverbs, I found five basic characteristics of lazy people:

1. Lazy people love sleep and hate alarm clocks.

In Proverbs, laziness and sleep are so closely linked that Solomon gives five warnings concerning the kind of sleep that crosses the line between rest and laziness. There is a difference between getting enough rest and getting too much sleep. While proper rest is healthy for the body, excess sleep is harmful in more ways than one.

- Too much sleep has a dulling effect. "As a door turns on its hinges, so a sluggard turns on his bed."[5] Excess sleep can become a hinge anchoring the body to the bed.[6]

- Too much sleep disables ambition. "Laziness brings on deep sleep, and the shiftless go hungry."[7]

- Too much sleep brings poverty. "Do not love sleep or you will grow poor; stay awake and you will have food to spare."[8]

- Too much sleep disappoints God. "How long will you lie there, you sluggard? When will you get up from your sleep?"[9]

- Too much sleep wastes opportunities. "He who gathers crops in summer is a prudent son, but he who sleeps during harvest is a disgraceful son."[10]

Normally, the hard-working person gets up when he wakes up; but when the lazy person wakes up he just rolls over. As a door on its hinges, there is much motion but no progress.

One man was filling out a job application that asked, "Does hard work bother you?" He answered, "Hard work does not bother me in the least. I can lie down next to it and go right to sleep." That is a lazy person. His god is sleep, his bed is his altar, and his body is the sacrifice he willingly offers. The lazy person is the ultimate couch potato. He can do anything as long as he is "lying down on the job."

Dad, to help your children conquer the alarm clock, have an agreed upon period of time they can sleep. Keeping in mind that younger kids need more sleep, expect your kids to go to bed at a reasonable hour so they can rise earlier. Have a rule that the "snooze button" is off limits. Enforce the discipline that when they wake up, they get up. On days they are not in school, have them finish any chores early in the day so the meat of the day can be given to enjoyable, leisurely activities.

2. Lazy people often start but rarely finish.

A lazy person will go hungry before he will work. As we noted a moment ago from Proverbs 19:15, Solomon said, "Laziness brings on deep sleep, and the shiftless go hungry."[11] Centuries later the apostle Paul was even more explicit: "For even when we were with you, we gave you this rule: 'The one who is unwilling to work shall not eat.'"[12]

> Lazy people will not work and therefore make no income; with no income they can buy no food and with no food they go hungry.

Lazy people will not work and therefore make no income; with no income they can buy no food and with no food they go hungry. But the problem does not stop there.

> The lazy man does not roast what he took in hunting,
> But diligence is man's precious possession.[13]

> A sluggard buries his hand in the dish;
>   he will not even bring it back to his mouth![14]

A lazy person loves buttered bread but is too lazy to butter it himself. If he kills an animal, he won't even clean the meat and cook it. He wants someone else not only to cook his meal, he wants someone else to feed it to him. The point is, he never starts a job; and if you give him one, he either won't finish it or he will do it only halfway.

We always reviewed our sons' schoolwork to make sure they were completing their assignments, turning in their homework on time, and doing their best work. We rewarded good grades monetarily to reinforce a job well done. If we agreed on quality control for a chore or other responsibility, and after fair warning the job was still unfinished or done poorly, they lost their reward. If one of my sons left for school without his room clean, he forfeited that day's portion of the allowance. We constantly reinforced the axiom that a job worth doing is worth doing well.

3. When lazy people say "later," they mean "never."

A lazy person is a master procrastinator. He never does today what he can put off until tomorrow, and he never does tomorrow what he can put off forever.

His favorite workday is tomorrow. That's why God is always asking him, "How long will you lie there, you sluggard? When will you get up from your sleep?"[15] If you are continually asking a person, "How long are you going to take off between jobs?" or "When are you going to look for another job?" you are talking to a lazy person.

> A child's favorite response to a command is often "in just a minute." Don't start buying it, or you will be paying for it forever.

A college student was trying to decide whether he should study. He grabbed a coin, flipped it, and said, "Heads, I'm going to the movies; tails, I'm going to watch TV. If it stands on its edge, I'm going to study." Some people are even too lazy to flip the coin. The sluggard is always going to "get around to doing the job," but he never gets around to getting around.

When to start a job is as important as when to complete it. A child's favorite response to a command is often "in just a minute." Don't start buying it, or you will be paying for it forever. Teach your kids that "now" means now and "finish" means don't turn the TV back on until the job is done.

4. Lazy people are big dreamers, but they do little.

"The craving of a sluggard will be the death of him, because his hands refuse to work," Solomon says.[16] The sluggard's favorite refrain is "One day..." You can just hear him now:

"One day I'm going to settle down and get a job."

"One day I'm going to own my own business."

"One day I'm going to hit the jackpot."

He wants what everybody wants—he just doesn't want to work for it. This thinking is one of the major reasons for the explosion of the welfare state. As Robert Hicks has wisely noted, "Feeling we're entitled to things without being willing to do the necessary labor to obtain them makes us a society of sluggards."[17]

> Dad, don't give even your small children everything. When they want certain things you think they should and could buy by doing chores, let them earn it and turn their dreams into reality.

The American dream for some has become the American nightmare for others because of their refusal to work to make those dreams come true. Dad, don't give even your small children everything. When they want certain things you think they should and could buy by doing chores, let them earn it and turn their dreams into reality.

5. Lazy people work hard...at defending their laziness.

"A sluggard is wiser in his own eyes than seven people who answer discreetly," Solomon says.[18] You will never convince a lazy person that they are lazy. Even if seven wise men tell him he is lazy, he will not admit it. He always has an excuse for why he cannot work. That is the meaning of Solomon's statement: "The way of the sluggard is blocked with thorns, but the path of the upright is a highway."[19] When the sluggard looks out the front door of life, he doesn't see a highway of opportunity; he only sees one big briar patch—or even a lion! "The sluggard says, 'There's a lion outside! I'll be killed in the public square!'"[20]

He sees a dark lining in every silver cloud, an obstacle in every opportunity. Though he cannot (will not) hold down a job, he always has a good excuse. The hours are too long; the pay is too little; the job is too hard; the people are too demanding—take your pick. (Don't worry if you don't like any of those; he has plenty more. Did you hear the one about the lion?)

Solomon said, "Sluggards do not plow in season; so at harvest time they look but find nothing."[21] It's always too hot or too cold or too wet or too dry to work. He always has an excuse. Thomas Edison, the epitome of a worker and the antithesis of a lazy person, said, "Opportunity is missed by most people because it is dressed in overalls and looks like work."[22] Old Benjamin Franklin was right when he said, "I never knew a man who was good at making excuses who was good at anything else."

Lazy people would rather make excuses than make a living. They are experts at doing nothing, calling it something, and defending it in the process.

Children have file cabinets full of excuses. I had to tell my kids on a few occasions, "It's time you learned the world doesn't want excuses; it wants results. Give your excuses while you are doing the job."

It's Crazy to Be Lazy

Lazy people represent *wasted talents*. The tragedy of this person is that he wastes the God-given abilities and gifts that are to be used not only to be productive but for the glory of his Creator. But his lifestyle does not harm only himself. "His work is a brother to him who is a great destroyer."[23] One writer explains how lazy people are destroyers:

That word "destroys" pulsates with liabilities. A lazy employee doesn't simply hold an organization back, he *destroys* its motivation and drive. A lazy player doesn't just weaken the team, he *destroys* its spirit and diminishes its will to win. A lazy pastor doesn't merely limit a church, he *destroys* its enthusiasm and its passion to win souls and meet needs. Before long, everyone must do more to compensate for the sluggard's negative influence.[24]

If you're a businessman, you know the truth of this statement: It is better to be shorthanded than to hire a sluggard; better to have nobody than a lazy body. Evidently, Solomon had suffered through a few sluggards on his payroll, for he said, "As vinegar to the teeth and smoke to the eyes, so are sluggards to those who send them."[25] Do you know how irritating vinegar is when taken straight, or how aggravating smoke is when it gets in your eyes? That's how irritating a lazy person is to the one who hires him. Whatever he does will take twice as long to finish and will either have to be done over or thrown out—at twice the cost. His presence on the job is worse than his absence.

Lazy people also represent *wasted resources*. A tragic picture is painted in Proverbs 24:30-31:

> I went past the field of a sluggard,
>   past the vineyard of someone who has no sense;
> thorns had come up everywhere,
>   the ground was covered with weeds,
>   and the stone wall was in ruins.

Where there should be a beautiful car with glistening chrome, clean windows, and spotless interior will instead be a rundown and rusted-out jalopy.

Worst of all, lazy people represent *wasted living*. Solomon's final warning to the sluggard is this:

> A little sleep, a little slumber,
>   a little folding of the hands to rest—
> and poverty will come on you like a thief
>   and scarcity like an armed man.[26]

We must always show compassion to the poor, especially those who are poor because of oppression, disaster, health, or conditions beyond their control. Nothing is more unchristian than ignoring this group of people. But we also need to help those who *can* help it. We need to train up our children to make a life for themselves, if at all possible.

One day your children will become husbands and fathers, wives and mothers. Your decision to ignore this principle with them will affect your grandchildren and their grandchildren. Because of our failures to raise up children with a proper work ethic, babies are hungry today, children are ill-clothed, and families lack a place to call home.

The Worth of Work

How do we teach our kids the value and the virtue of work? Solomon's simple solution to slothfulness is study. Solomon took his children out to a pile of dirt one day and made them study... the ant.

> Go to the ant, you sluggard;
>   consider its ways and be wise!
> It has no commander,
>   no overseer or ruler,
> yet it stores its provisions in summer
>   and gathers its food at harvest.[27]

How wise and brilliant Solomon was! For no creature on earth personifies a good work ethic more than the ant. Consider only a few admirable qualities we learn from ants:

1. We should be workers you can count on.

While the queen ant is the center of attention and the mother of most of the ants in the colony, she is not the chief ruler. Instead, the work and survival of the colony is ensured by soldier ants. These servant leaders are older ants who begin each new activity in the colony by doing the work themselves. Younger ants then imitate the servant-leaders and join in the work. There are no supervisors, chiefs, or officers among the ants.[28] That explains Solomon's comment that ants have "no commander, no overseer or ruler."

The ant is a self-starter, a picture of the diligent person described in Proverbs 10:4: "Lazy hands make for poverty, but diligent hands bring wealth." The diligent person in Proverbs is the opposite of the lazy person. He is "characterized by steady, earnest, and energetic effort."[29] He wants to work, make a difference, and contribute to the flourishing of society. What the ant does by instinct, humans should do by desire.

2. We should be workers who stay on task.

The job of most ants is to find food so the colony can eat. Their hunger drives them to their job. They either work or die. The ant knows hunger is not all bad. As Solomon observed, "The appetite of laborers works for them; their hunger drives them on."[30] Hunger is God's motivating force to labor. That stomach growl to the lazy person is God's way of saying, "Get a job and make a way for yourself."

The ant never sees work as menial or beneath his dignity. Whether it is moving dirt or carrying breadcrumbs, he merrily does his job. How unlike many people today! Someone has remarked that if you want to keep teenagers out of hot water, put dirty dishes in it.

Dad, one of the greatest lessons you will ever teach your kids is that all work is valuable. All work can and should be done for the glory of God. The sum of the matter is found in this simple statement: "In all labor there is profit."[31]

> Every honorable vocation, regardless of what it is,
> is a calling from God.

One day your kids will decide what their life's vocation is going to be. As they make this crucial decision, you would do well to teach them that the very word *vocation* comes from the Latin word *vocare,* meaning "to call." Every honorable vocation, regardless of what it is, is a calling from God.[32]

Martin Luther King Jr. rightly declared, "Not all men are called to specialized or professional jobs; even fewer to the heights of genius in the arts and sciences; many are called to be laborers in factories, fields and streets. But no work is insignificant."[33]

Before we implemented the allowance system in our house, we sat our children down and handed them a contract. The following is a sample contract I used with my two younger sons:

Contract with Character on Chores

1. Daily chores
    a. make up bed/clean room
    b. clean up bathroom of your towels, clothes, etc.
    c. be at breakfast at 7:30 a.m. for family devotions

2. Do jobs asked with positive attitude

3. Additional chores—Jonathan:

      a. vacuum study/dust study once a week

      b. dishwasher twice a week

      c. vacuum once every other week

      d. clean bathrooms once a month

4. Additional chores—Joshua

      a. collect garbage twice a week

      b. dishwasher twice a week

      c. vacuum once every other week

      d. clean bathrooms once a month

5. Allowance paid every Friday

6. 10 percent must be set aside for tithe / 10 percent must be set aside for savings / other money should be used wisely and with counsel of parents.

Signed: _____ Jonathan Merritt

Signed: _____ Joshua Merritt

Signed: _____ Mom and Dad

I'm big on contracts because they clarify expectations to avoid misunderstandings. And they teach integrity and faithfulness in keeping your word. (Not to mention teaching the importance of being careful of what you sign.)

3. We should be workers who do our jobs well.

Consider this: A leaf-cutting ant may carry up to fifty times its own weight for more than a hundred yards. That is equivalent to a two-hundred-pound man carrying five tons on his back for a distance of seventeen miles. In a single summer, a large colony of ants may excavate thirty thousand to forty thousand pounds of earth to make its nest, and carry five thousand pounds of material back into the nest for food.[34]

The ant may make as many as four round trips a day to food

sources, which may be more than four hundred feet from the nest. That is roughly equivalent to a man's walking sixty-eight miles. If the ant had the stride of a man, it would be capable of bursts of speed in excess of sixty-five miles an hour and would walk normally at a speed of twenty miles per hour.[35] (And you think you have it rough.) One thing about an ant you can always count on: he always gives his best and pulls his share of the load.

Dad, instruct your kids that their reputation will never rise above their work ethic and how people see them as workers. I remember when my two oldest sons got their first jobs. The eldest, James Jr., worked in our church doing maintenance, and Jonathan worked for a man in our church doing yard work. People have paid me compliments about my sons before, but I don't think I have ever been prouder than when both of their bosses came to me, without any prodding, to tell me that my boys were hard workers who could be trusted to do a job well.

4. We should be workers who finish our jobs.

The ant literally dies working, and so should we. I have searched the Bible, and I have never found the contemporary concept of retirement. You may retire from a *job,* but you never retire from *work.* As long as you live, God always has work He wants you to do.

You dads might want to share this with your fathers and grandfathers: Harvard University commissioned a study of two groups of its graduates. One group of one hundred men retired at age sixty-five, and another group worked to age seventy-five. In the first group, seven out of eight were dead by age seventy-five. But in the group that kept working, only one in eight had died. The researchers concluded that retiring too early reduces longevity.[36]

Dad, the greatest example of work you will ever find is Jesus Christ Himself, who said to the Father at the end of His three-year ministry: "I have brought you glory on earth by finishing the work you gave me to do."[37] Has it ever occurred to you that salvation is available because Jesus proved Himself to be a faithful laborer who stayed on task until the job was done? Teach your kids to do the same. They will be happier and so will you.

Taking Your Leisure, Doing Your Best

Solomon had no problem with leisure. Every worker needs rest, for a laborer rested and refreshed will be a better laborer. The average American will work 1787 hours each year, and too few will take adequate time to rest.[38] Humans need a strong rest ethic as much as they need a strong work ethic.

The contrast in Proverbs is not between labor and leisure but between labor and laziness. Dads, when you come home, be home. Turn the smartphone off. Stop checking email. One of the most damaging things a parent can do is to be physically present but emotionally inaccessible. Learn to be present and leave your work at the office. In this way, you'll teach your children that work is important—very important—but it is not everything.

Today, my eldest son is a thriving attorney. My middle son is a renowned writer. And my youngest son is a successful pilot. They have each chosen their path in life—quite different from each other—but they've maintained a strong work ethic in their respective fields. I never tried to coerce them to pursue a particular career path, but I always wanted them to do their best at whatever path they chose. This is something all kids need to hear.

I once gave everyone on my staff a framed copy of the following saying by Walt Disney, which explains why the Disney brand is still so magical today: "Do what you do so well, that those who see you do what you do are going to come back to see you do it again, and tell others that they should see you do what you do."[39]

A tall order? You bet. But it works, it's biblical, and it's what we dads are called to do. Dad, whatever else you teach your kids about work, teach them to:

- Work hard.
- Finish the job.
- Learn to rest.
- Do their best.

If they learn those lessons well and put them into practice, you won't have to teach them much about success. It will already be their close friend and constant companion.

8

Strive to Be Fiscally Fit

*"The trouble with the rat race is that even
if you win, you're still a rat."*

JANE WAGNER, *THE SEARCH FOR SIGNS OF INTELLIGENT LIFE IN THE UNIVERSE*

My children came of age during the 1990s, a time of great prosperity in America. None in that time could have foreseen the falling, flaming towers of September 11, 2001. And none could have predicted the economic depression that would follow closely behind. Our world today is much different from the nineties, not to mention the fifties and sixties when I grew up. But one constant remains: the way you handle your finances is paramount.

I'm grateful that I did not overlook this constant during that period of economic prosperity. It would have been easy. (After all, everybody seems to agree that money is unimportant—until they don't have any.) Luckily, I instilled in my children a value for money and for stewarding it wisely, and I'm glad I did.

The Scriptures are chock-full of teaching about money. Howard Dayton, the founder of Crown Ministries, has counted about 500 verses in the Bible on prayer, but more than 2350 on how to handle money and possessions.[1] But too often when we begin to think about money management, we go to our financial advisor instead of searching God's heart.

Given the prolific teachings on money in the Bible, it may not surprise you to find that Solomon had much to say about the matter. After all, he was the richest man who ever lived in addition to the wisest. In this letter to dads, the ancient king talks often to those he calls "the rich." If you're like me, your first impulse is to overlook this phrase as if it refers to someone who makes more money than you do. But don't check out just yet. The amount of hard cash lost each year in the United States amounts to about seventy-five dollars per capita, while the total average income for most of this planet comes to about sixty-nine dollars per person annually. In other words, the average American *loses* more money each year than almost anyone else in the world *earns*.[2] The average American is far more wealthy than he cares to admit.

Money is something we all live with and think we cannot live without. Money may come from *how* you make it, but money is *what* you make it, as this anonymous poem shows:

> Dug from the mountainside
> or washing in the glen,
> Servant am I, or master of men.
> Earn me, I bless you;
> steal me, I curse you!
> Grasp me and hold me,
> a fiend will possess you.
> Lie for me, die for me,
> covet me, take me—
> angel or devil
> I'm just what you make me.

Money is like nitroglycerin: Handling it is not morally wrong, but it is extremely risky (especially if you do not know what you're doing). It seems as if everywhere you look, there is a warning label of some kind on toys, cigarettes, diet soft drinks, and even air bags. Perhaps it would be a good idea to put a warning label on dollar bills, certificates of deposit, and credit cards, for nothing has been the ruin of more people, marriages, and friendships than the failure to handle money properly.

> The ability to handle money today can make or break many a family. A Gallup poll indicates that the lack of money is the biggest challenge families face today, followed by health care.

The ability to handle money today can (and does) make or break many a family. A Gallup poll indicates that the lack of money is the biggest challenge families face today, followed by health care.[3] And yet, very few Americans have a clue about how to manage money. That's why the average American household today carries in excess of fifteen thousand dollars of credit card debt, according to the Federal Reserve.[4] Indeed, people who don't know how to manage money have helped people who do—like Dave Ramsey—make a lot of it. Therefore, taking some time to explore how to prepare your children to handle this wonderful but dangerous commodity is worthwhile.

How You Should Make Money

Solomon assumes that people will work to make money, so there is nothing wrong with earning it. As Moses reminded the children of Israel, it is God who is the real moneymaker. He said to them, "Remember the LORD your God, for it is he who gives you the ability to produce wealth."[5] It stands to reason that if the

Lord is the one who enables us to make money, then He expects us to do it in some measure.

Yet Solomon tells us there is a right way and a wrong way to make money. First, it should come by *hard work*. He writes,

> Lazy hands make for poverty,
>> but diligent hands bring wealth.[6]

> Those who work their land will have abundant food,
>> but those who chase fantasies have no sense.[7]

> Dishonest money dwindles away,
>> but whoever gathers money little by little makes it
>> grow.[8]

Both labor and management are to make money. Labor helps management make a profit, while management provides labor with wages. Neither a profit well-earned nor a wage honestly made displease the Lord.

But money is also to be earned by *honest work*. There are grave warnings given to those who get their money dishonestly. There is a warning against *oppressing the poor*. "One who oppresses the poor to increase his wealth and one who gives gifts to the rich— both come to poverty," Solomon says.[9]

He also warns against cheating innocent people. This can be done by charging excess interest on loans or artificially inflating prices. "Whoever increases wealth by taking interest or profit from the poor amasses it for another, who will be kind to the poor," Solomon writes.[10]

As I used to recite to my sons,
"Winners never cheat, and cheaters never win."
Money must be made ethically and morally.

A final warning is sounded about dishonest business practices, such as padding expense accounts. Listen to Eugene Peterson's translation of Proverbs 20:10 (MSG): "Switching price tags and padding the expense account are two things God hates."

There are many more ways to gain money unethically and illegally, but as I used to recite to my sons, "Winners never cheat, and cheaters never win." Money must be made ethically and morally.

Yet God is concerned with far more than the making of money. His greater concerns are the managing of money and the mastering of money. My wife and I began teaching our kids early the principles of industry, honesty, and responsibility. Here are a few methods we used which I recommend to you:

Give your kids some jobs early on, without pay, such as making their beds, picking up their toys, and cleaning their rooms. Inspect their room each time, encouraging them as much as possible, but also letting them know the standard of quality you expect. This will teach them the value of work, the fulfillment of doing a job well, and the discipline of following the commands of someone in authority over them.

As your kids get older, choose some jobs they are capable of doing (polishing shoes, washing the car, vacuuming the floor) *and settle on fair compensation*. This will begin to instruct them in the value of money and reinforce the rewards of a job well done. Again, have an understood standard of quality and don't pay until the job is completed properly.

Don't give freebie allowances nor teach your children to expect them. Rather, teach them that money is earned through working for it. There is nothing wrong with giving your child money out of love or as a reward (such as for good grades), but kids must learn the relationship between honest labor and just compensation.

Avoid anything that instills a sense of entitlement. Teach your children that no human owes them anything and that money is to be primarily earned as fruit from the tree of honest labor. Don't be like the distraught father who was venting some of his frustrations about the conflicts between him and his son over the use of their family car. He said to his friend, "I'm sick and tired of arguing with my teenage son about borrowing the car. Next time, I'm just going to take it when I want it."

Mastered by Money v. Master of Money

You are either master over your money or a slave to it; there is no in-between.[11] In Proverbs, we glean ten keys to helping you master your money—lessons you can pass on to your children that will be "worth their weight in gold":

1. Being poor may be a problem, but being rich isn't the solution.

The desire for wealth is a natural human impulse, but riches aren't all they are cracked up to be. "The rich can pay a ransom for their lives," says Solomon, "but the poor won't even get threatened."[12] For the rich, the bad news is that they are worth kidnapping. The good news is, they are able to pay the ransom. For the poor, the bad news is that they are not worth kidnapping. The good news is, they don't have to worry about a ransom.

> You are either master over your money or a slave to it; there is no in-between.

Solomon used this example to illustrate the real danger of money: Money solves problems, but it also creates them. Patrick Morley put it well: "Money is intoxicating. It is an opiate that addicts us as easily and completely as the iron grip of alcohol or narcotics...Money enslaves men—it will work you till you die and, after it has conquered your poor soul, its haunting laughter can be heard howling through the chambers of hell."[13]

There is no penalty for prosperity nor is there a premium on poverty. Great wealth brings great worries, headaches, temptations, and difficulties that the not-so-rich don't have to bother with.

2. There's a difference between needy and greedy.

"Such are the paths of all who go after ill-gotten gain; it takes away the life of those who get it," Solomon writes.[14] We Americans pledge allegiance to "one nation under God," and then we often live as if we believe in "one nation under greed."[15]

A greedy man is like the heroin addict: it takes a hit to satisfy him, but the effect soon wears off, and he needs another. When John D. Rockefeller was the richest man in the world, he was asked by an employee, "Mr. Rockefeller, how much money is enough?" To which Rockefeller replied, "Just a little bit more, son, just a little bit more."

Larry Burkett advised parents to let their children know (at an appropriate age) the family's income, living expenses, taxes, and giving habits. This will not only help them develop a realistic attitude about expenses, thrift, and stewardship, but it will also enable them to see why being content with the family's style of living is necessary.[16]

I want to shout out a caution here to dads and moms. You can teach and talk all you want, but if you live the typical American lifestyle—consumeristic and materialistic—your kids will adapt and adopt accordingly.

If *newer* and *better* are the driving words behind how you spend your money, tame that greed by being content with having what you need. As a Greek sage once said, "To whom a little is not enough, nothing is enough."

3. Family comes before money, both in the dictionary and in life.

"The greedy bring ruin to their households, but the one who hates bribes will live," the wise king said.[17] Anyone who puts work, career, money, or possessions above family is asking for big trouble. At one time, J. Paul Getty owned an estate that exceeded four billion dollars in net worth. He was considered, in his day, the richest and most "successful" man on planet Earth. Years ago, the *Los Angeles Times* quoted something Getty wrote in his autobiography:

> "I have never been given to envy, save for the envy I feel toward those people who have the ability to make a marriage work and endure happily. It's an art I have never been able to master. My record: five marriages, five divorces. In short, five failures…"

> He termed the memories of his relationship with his five sons "painful." Much of his pain has been passed on with his money. His most treasured offspring, Timothy, a frail child born when Getty was fifty-three, died in 1958 at the age of twelve, of surgical complications after a sickly life, spent mostly separated from his father who was forever away on business.

> Other members of the Getty family also suffered from tragic circumstances. A grandson, J. Paul Getty III, was kidnapped and held for a ransom of $2.9 million. When Getty refused to pay, they held the boy for five months and eventually cut off his right ear. Getty's oldest son apparently committed suicide amid strange circumstances. Another son, Gordon Paul Getty, has been described as living a tortured existence. He was ridiculed in correspondence by his father and was the least favored son. Similar sorrow has followed other members of this unfortunate family.[18]

I am not trying to imply that being rich guarantees family problems, nor do I believe that every wealthy person has sacrificed his family to become so. I am simply saying that Solomon was right when he said that putting money first and family second can and most probably will make you nothing more than a wealthy failure.

> Money is a terrible substitute for time, attention, and affection. Don't adopt a lifestyle that forces you to sacrifice your family on the altar of material needs.

Dad, whenever possible, attend that child's ball game, recital, or school event. Let your children know early and often, both in word and deed, where your priorities are and where they are on that list. Money is a terrible substitute for time, attention, and affection. Don't adopt a lifestyle that forces you to sacrifice your family on the altar of material needs.

4. Be satisfied with needs, rather than consumed by wants.

In the brilliant section of Proverbs penned by the mysterious Agur (Proverbs 30), we find a prayer loaded with financial wisdom.

> "Two things I ask of you, LORD;
>   do not refuse me before I die:
> Keep falsehood and lies far from me;
>   give me neither poverty nor riches,
>   but give me only my daily bread.
> Otherwise, I may have too much and disown you
>   and say, 'Who is the Lord?'
> Or I may become poor and steal,
>   and so dishonor the name of my God."[19]

Agur did not want to be either in the upper class or the lower class. He wanted to be only middle class. He didn't want to drive a Rolls Royce, and he didn't really want to walk; he wanted only a reliable used car. In his own way, it seems, Agur was a rich man.

He was like a man I heard of who lived on a very modest income. This man was talking one day to his boss, a greedy, grasping businessman who was always trying to get more and more. They were sitting together at lunch, and the employee looked at the business tycoon and said, "I am richer than you are."

"How do you figure that?" the businessman said with a sneer.

"Because I have all the money I want, and you don't."

You can be rich in one of two ways: either in how much you have or in how little you want. The debt crisis in America is primarily caused by greed and covetousness, which is simply the failure to be satisfied with enough. When you kill the tumor of greed, you destroy the cancer of covetousness.

Dad, let me give you a couple of practical suggestions for you and your kids.

Take your children on a mission trip overseas and let them experience different cultures and see how the rest of the world lives. My sons got to see everything from Brazilian kids in barrios to Middle Eastern kids begging for money on the street. Each time, there was a heightened appreciation for how great they had things at home.

Periodically involve your children in some type of project for needy people not only to teach them compassion but to help them to be more content with what they have. You never truly realize how much you have until you see how much others don't have.

5. Money will never satisfy your deepest needs or even all your wants.

You might think that people would grow happier as a culture grows more affluent, but consider this observation written several years ago:

In 1957, as John Galbraith was about to describe us as *the affluent society,* our per-person income, expressed in today's dollars, was less than $8,000. Today it is $16,000, making us The Doubly Affluent Society. Compared to 1957, we have twice as many cars per person; we have microwave ovens, color TVs, VCRs, air conditioners, answering machines, and $12 billion a year worth of brand-name athletic shoes.

So are we happier than we were thirty-five years ago? We are not. In 1957, thirty-five percent of Americans told *The National Opinion Research Center* they were "very happy." In 1991, with doubled American affluence, thirty-one percent said the same. Judged by soaring rates of depression, the quintupling of the violent crime rate since 1960, the doubling of the divorce rate, the slight decline in marital happiness among the marital survivors, and the tripling of the teen suicide rate, we are richer and unhappier. How can we avoid the shocking conclusion: Economic growth in affluent countries gives little boost to human morale.[20]

Neither you nor your children will ever learn a greater lesson than this: Money is not guaranteed to make you happier; in fact, it may make you sadder.

We are even wealthier today than when that was written, but we are no happier and perhaps we have grown less content. Dad, neither you nor your children will ever learn a greater lesson than this: Money is not guaranteed to make you happier; in fact, it may make you sadder.

My happiest times with my sons were not our most expensive

vacations or a time when someone made a large purchase. They were those simple moments when we were just enjoying each other's company. Even today there is nothing I enjoy more than when my sons and I take a Saturday and cruise over to Athens to watch our beloved Georgia Bulldogs play. It still makes me feel like a young father, taking me back to those days when I was just hanging out with my three best friends, tailgating, talking dad-son stuff, and basking in their company.

Dad, after you've rented that video, popped the popcorn, and enjoyed the fire together as a family, take the opportunity to tell your kids that the experience you shared and the memories you built are far more valuable to you than a bigger bank account, a higher position, or any other material blessing. They need to hear this from you.

6. Overtime is not worth the time-and-a-half.

> Do not wear yourself out to get rich;
>   do not trust your own cleverness.
> Cast but a glance at riches, and they are gone,
>   for they will surely sprout wings
>   and fly off to the sky like an eagle.[21]

The security of money is a mirage. Elvis Presley's stepbrother, Rick, is a dear friend of mine. The first time we met years ago, he told me the number one question people would ask him after Elvis died was, "How much did Elvis leave behind?"

Rick just flashed that wide-faced, show-stopping grin of his and said, "James, you know what I tell them? 'He left it all.'"

I don't care how much money you make, how much money you save, how much money you invest, and how much money you keep. Eventually, either your money will leave you, or you will leave it.

I don't care how much money you make, how much money you save, how much money you invest, and how much money you keep. Eventually, either your money will leave you, or you will leave it. So never motivate your children to make wealth the number one goal in their life.

My mentor, Pastor Adrian Rogers, once heard someone say, "It's all right to make all the money you can as long as you make it honestly." He responded, "That is wrong. If you are making all the money you can, that means you are making money when you should be spending time with your family, with your friends, or with God." The way you spend your time is more important than how you spend your money. Spend time wisely on your spouse, children, friends, and your Maker.

7. Believe that giving is more important than getting...then give.

Solomon went against the grain of all financial thinking when he said, in effect, that the key to getting is not getting but giving:

> Honor the LORD with your wealth,
>> with the firstfruits of all your crops;
> then your barns will be filled to overflowing,
>> and your vats will brim over with new wine.[22]

Proverbs was written to an agrarian culture, and the income of the original readers was tied to crops and livestock. Whenever a farmer or rancher reaped a harvest or birthed some lambs, he would take the first sheaf of the harvest or the firstborn of the flock and commit it to the temple and to the Lord. In fact, the firstborn of his children was also committed to the service of the Lord. These were called "firstfruits."

By giving away his firstfruits, a person acknowledged God's goodness and sovereignty. By committing the firstfruits to the Lord, the farmer was confessing that all he had came from God and belonged to God. God demands first place in every area of our lives. The firstborn child would learn by this experience the place that God held in the family.

When a person gives God the first cut of his money, he acknowledges that God is first in this area of his life. This in turn gives confidence that God will provide the basic necessities. Solomon instructs us to give God the firstfruits, not the leftovers.

Arthur DeMoss was a spiritual giant and benefactor who gave millions to God's work and left behind a foundation to carry on his legacy. Mr. DeMoss said that to be successful you should give God the first dime out of every dollar, the first hour out of every day, and the first day out of every week. Dad, that is great advice for any father to pass along to his children.

Unfortunately, as wealthy as Americans are, God mostly gets the leftovers—and with many people, He doesn't even get the crumbs. Households earning more than $100,000 a year in 2011 gave on average 3.1 percent of their income to charity, while households with incomes of less than $10,000 gave 5.5 percent.

What is even sadder is that as America becomes more prosperous, she's also becoming more stingy. In 1933, at the depth of the Great Depression, church members gave an estimated 3.3 percent of their disposable income to the church. In 2009 that figure was 2.38 percent.

Gangaram Mahes is a criminal but a most extraordinary one. Although he has been arrested nearly three dozen times, you would never be frightened by his presence—that is, unless you own a classy restaurant. This immigrant from Guyana is known as a "serial eater" because he loves eloquent dining but doesn't have the budget to pay for it. Rather than deny his appetite, he simply walks into a fine restaurant, orders the best meal on the menu, the finest liquors, and the most expensive desserts. He then eats and drinks to his heart's content, and when the check arrives, simply informs the waiter he is neither able nor willing to pay the bill. The police then come and arrest him, and he ends up with at least a few days of free meals in jail.[23]

Our world today is filled with people who eat and drink God's blessings in life but fail to give back even a meager tip to God and others. Dad, I encourage you to urge, perhaps even insist, that from the first money your child earns, he gives the firstfruits to the Lord. Teach your children generosity early on. Also, let *them* give it rather than give for them. This teaches the child not only the duty of stewardship but the joy of giving.

8. Cash out or you will cash in.

What does this principle mean? Except for a house, a car (maybe), or an absolute emergency, *pay cash or don't buy it.* There are too many people for whom finances have become a matter of "life and debt." Today people can be divided into three classes:

- The Haves
- The Have-Nots
- The Have-Not-Paid-for-What-They-Haves

> Except for a house, a car, or an absolute emergency, *pay cash or don't buy it.* There are too many people for whom finances have become a matter of "life and debt."

Americans are the most indebted people on earth. Consider the following:

- Total US credit card debt is more than 8 times larger than it was just thirty years ago.
- Consumers owe lenders a record 19 percent of their disposable income, not including mortgage and

home equity loans or auto leases. Credit card debt
alone is 7.5 percent.

- The average cardholder carries a balance of $3,900,
  and only about a third pay their credit card bills in full
  each month.

- Americans now owe more than $904 billion on stu-
  dent loans, which is a new all-time high.

- Average household debt in the United States has now
  reached a level of 136 percent of average household
  income. In China, average household debt is only 17
  percent of average household income.

- A staggering 25 percent of all American adults now
  have a credit score below 599.

What we call credit is not credit at all; it's really the opposite. Suppose you wanted to buy a refrigerator from an appli-
ance store. You don't have the money right now, but the owner
agrees to let you drop by once a month and pay one hundred
dollars toward the price. He keeps the refrigerator but doesn't
charge you any interest or layaway fee. When the refrigerator is
paid for, it's yours.

Every time you pay one hundred dollars, you come away with
a receipt showing a *credit* toward the purchase price. Your account
is *credited* once a month, and when the *credit* paid equals the purchase price, the refrigerator is yours. Now *that* is credit.

But what society calls credit is really debt. A "credit line" of
one thousand dollars is actually a debt potential for that amount.
So when you buy something "on credit," you are actually buying
it "on debt." It would be better to call a credit card a debt card.[24]

I see bumper stickers frequently that read, "I owe, I owe, so
off to work I go!" I have a feeling that the message is more serious

than it is funny. Someone has described a modern American as a person who drives a bank-financed car, over a bond-financed road, on gasoline he bought with a credit card, to a department store to open another charge account so he can fill his house that is mortgaged to the Savings and Loan, with furniture that has been purchased on an installment plan.

Having said that, understand that the Bible does not condemn debt; the Bible *cautions* about debt. Solomon makes an oft-quoted statement about borrowing money that is often misunderstood and misused: "The rich rule over the poor, and the borrower is slave to the lender."[25]

Contrary to popular opinion, this verse does not condemn debt; it merely states a fact. The borrower is a servant to the lender by the fact that he is bound to pay the lender what he owes him. He has an obligation he must fulfill. He has to pay what he owes. It is not wicked to borrow money; it is wicked to borrow money *and not repay it.* As Solomon's father said, "The wicked borrow and do not repay."[26]

Incidentally, if your kids ever want to borrow money from you, perhaps against a future allowance or a future chore to be done, let them (if it is for a good reason). But write down the terms of the agreement, when the money is to be repaid, and the penalty for a late payment (unless there are extenuating circumstances, such as illness). This will help them learn the real world of borrowing and the discipline of timely debt repayment.

Still, there are circumstances where I believe debt is wrong and should be avoided:

- Avoid debt when it is beyond your ability to repay it on time.

- Avoid debt when it prevents you from giving to God and others.

- Avoid debt when the burden is so heavy you cannot save for the future.

- Avoid debt if it puts your family under financial pressure.

- Avoid debt if it is used to pay for luxuries.

- Avoid debt if it is generated by cosigning a note.[27]

You can borrow for *necessities,* but you should pay cash for *luxuries.* If at all possible, *pay cash or don't buy it.* A great way to teach your children this principle is to have them buy something they want with money they earn. It doesn't have to be much (perhaps ten dollars to buy a toy). Then let them buy it with their own money, impressing them with the fact that the thing bought is totally theirs and they owe no one.

9. Save for that rainy day.

Consider the ant who "stores its provisions in summer and gathers its food at harvest."[28] The ant is always getting ready for the winter months when no work can be done. If only people had that much ant sense. I was astonished to read that eighty-five out of one hundred Americans end up with less than $250 in cash savings when they reach sixty-five. Can you believe that America's savings per household is $4201—less than one-third that of Germany and less than one-tenth that of Japan? Anyone can *spend* money. The wise man *saves* some as well.

Keep in mind that *debt is the opposite of savings.* The reason is simple: *You either earn interest or you pay interest.* I know it's difficult for many families to save, but I want to encourage you to begin right now. If we got by with less today, we could save up more for tomorrow.

10. Don't keep up with the Joneses (or anyone else, for that matter).

> Things aren't evil. Money isn't evil.
> Teach your children to enjoy some of the things that money can buy without sacrificing the things that money can never buy.

"One person pretends to be rich, yet has nothing; another pretends to be poor, yet has great wealth," Solomon said.[29] You can be spared a lot of anxiety and sleepless nights if you will just learn that not only should you refuse to keep up with the Joneses, but if you ever *do* catch up with them, they will just refinance. As humorist Will Rogers said, "People borrow money they don't have, to buy things they don't need, to impress people they don't even like." You will never be satisfied with what you have until you learn to be satisfied with what others have.

Remember What Is Important

The overarching habit of fiscal fitness is remembering what's important and what's not. What you are is more important than what you have. As Solomon said, "Better the poor whose walk is blameless than the rich whose ways are perverse."[30] And most importantly, what God sees in you is more important that what you have. As Solomon said, "Better a little with the fear of the LORD than great wealth with turmoil."[31]

Things aren't evil. Money isn't evil. Teach your children to enjoy some of the things money can buy without sacrificing the things money can never buy. The greatest joys in life are not for sale. As Socrates once said after looking around the Athenian marketplace: "What a lot of things there are a man can do without."[32]

Dads, there are a lot of things we can do without. And almost as many that we *should* do without. Great wealth is one of them. What we cannot afford to live without is a family filled with love, a close relationship with our children, and a life well-lived for God's glory. There is a great cost to money, and often the price is too high to pay. If you want your children to be fiscally fit, make sure they know what is important. If you do this, you will die a wealthy man and you will have been a successful father.

9

Be Good and Be Godly

*"Could I climb to the highest place in Athens, I
would lift my voice and proclaim:
'Fellow citizens, why do you turn and
scrape every stone to gather wealth,
and take so little care of your children,
to whom one day you must relinquish it all?'"*

SOCRATES

I f life takes its natural course, I'll pass from this world twenty
or so years from now. However I go—peacefully in my sleep,
wrestling with a painful disease, or some other means—I will
stand before my Creator and offer an account for how I lived. I
will explain why I didn't always love my wife as well as I should
have, and why I often failed as a pastor. I will justify the decisions I made as an impulsive college student, and those I made as
a graying grandfather. The older I get, the more often I consider
what this experience will be like.

I'm not sure what that moment will look or feel like. I don't
know how it will make me feel to relive life in such a way. But one
thing I do know: when it comes to offering God an account of my
time as a parent, I will not have to explain why I never taught my
children the difference between right and wrong. I didn't want

to raise just good sons but also godly sons. I'm afraid too many dads today miss the difference between the two. They abdicate their responsibility to develop the spiritual lives of their children.

Proverbs is actually the first of a trilogy of biblical books written by Solomon; the last (chronologically) is Ecclesiastes. Most likely, this work was written when the king was in the later stages of his life. Like Proverbs, it is a distillation of divine wisdom as it has been tested in the crucible of life.

I have read it at least two or three times a year for as long as I can remember, but I guess my sensitivity to Solomon's writing as a father in Proverbs caused me to see something recently that I had never seen before. It was a discovery that both amazed and excited me.

Solomon's last book could almost be characterized as one long, negative commentary on the vanity or emptiness of life. Whether it comes to the intellectual pursuit of knowledge, the physical pursuit of pleasure, or the material pursuit of wealth, this grizzled veteran could say, "Been there, done that, and it's the same ol' same ol'."

> At the end of his life and literary career, Solomon was still writing and talking to his son. He may have been old enough to be a grandfather, but he was still young enough to think like a father.

I was reading his book, coasting along on cruise control in the final chapter, when *it happened.* All of a sudden my eyes widened and the zoom lens of my vision focused on two words: "*my son.*"[1] Do you see? At the end of his life and literary career, Solomon was still writing and talking to his son. He may have been old enough to be a grandfather, but he was still young enough to think like a father.

Years earlier Solomon had written to his son on every vital

subject, ranging from sex and money to alcohol and work. Now, penning his last divinely inspired thoughts, he wrapped up his life's message with the words every congregation loves to hear the preacher say during his Sunday morning message: "here is the conclusion of the matter."[2]

What is the "conclusion"? It is the life message every dad must pass on to his children: "Fear God and keep his commandments, for this is the duty of all mankind."[3] In other words, Solomon was saying, "Son, when it comes to God, trust and obey." Dad, whatever else you teach your kids, give to your kids, or do for your kids, you must lead them to love, trust, and obey God...or else your fatherhood, from an eternal perspective, has been in vain.

It is no coincidence that Solomon ended his last book where he began his first one (Proverbs 1:7), by admonishing his son to fear the Lord. Love for God begins with the reverence that is due Him. In turn, the person who learns to fear the Lord will pay attention to His Word and obey it. That, in sum, is the life of wisdom: fearing God and doing His will.

> Fatherhood is more than conceiving, feeding, clothing, educating, and sending children out on their own. Dads have the responsibility of preparing their children for their eternal destiny of meeting God.

Like me, the aged king was thinking about the afterlife. "For God will bring every deed into judgment, including every hidden thing, whether it is good or evil," he writes.[4] He knew that fatherhood is more than conceiving, feeding, clothing, educating, and sending children out on their own. Solomon knew dads have the responsibility of preparing their children for their eternal destiny of meeting God. We must make sure our earthly children are prepared to meet their heavenly Creator.

Morality Matters

In *Why Johnny Can't Tell Right from Wrong,* William Kilpatrick argues that part of the reason for this moral confusion lies in the influence of powerful myths (some old, some new) that dominate our thinking about child rearing. He identified these myths:

The myth of the "good bad boy." American literature and film loves to portray "bad" boys as essentially lovable and happy. Tom Sawyer and Buster Brown are examples from the past; the various lovable brats featured in film and television are contemporary examples. This strand in the American tradition has such a powerful hold on the imagination that the word *obedience* is very nearly a dirty word in the American vocabulary. The myth of the "good bad boy" is connected to...

The myth of natural goodness. This is the idea that virtue will take care of itself if children are just allowed to grow in their own way.

The myth of expert knowledge. In recent decades parents have deferred to professional authority in the matter of raising their children. Unfortunately, the vast majority of child-rearing experts subscribe to the myth of natural goodness mentioned above. So much emphasis has been placed on the unique creative and spontaneous nature of children, that parents have come to feel that child rearing means adjusting themselves to their children, rather than having children learn to adjust to the requirements of family life.

The myth that moral problems are psychological. This myth is connected to all of the above. In this view, behavior problems are seen as problems in self-esteem, or as the result of unmet psychological needs. The old-fashioned idea that most behavior problems are the result of sheer "willfulness" on the part of children doesn't occur to the average child expert. If you look in the index of a typical child-rearing book, you will find that a great many pages are devoted to "self-esteem," but you are not likely to find the word "character" anywhere.

The myth that parents don't have the right to instill their values in their children. Once again the standard dogma here is that children must create their own values. But, of course, children have precious little chance to do that since the rest of the culture has no qualms about imposing values. Does it make sense for parents to remain neutral bystanders when everyone else—from scriptwriters, to entertainers, to advertisers, to teachers—insists on selling their values to our children?[5]

I have spent my life excavating Solomon's writings, and what I've found offers a resounding no to the last question Mr. Kilpatrick raises. The king knew that morality matters, which is why he spent so much time talking about matters of morality.

In Proverbs, Solomon compares wisdom to silver taken from a mine and to hidden treasures: "If you look for [wisdom] as for silver and search for it as for hidden treasure."[6] This book contains nuggets of wisdom I have quarried with my own shovel from the mineshaft of God's Word. I have tried not only to share with fellow dads eternal truths that can be practically applied in the life of their children, but also destroy some myths that have been perpetrated in our society concerning the rearing of our children. I have tried to motivate you to be proactive in encouraging the development of honesty, reliability, respect, godliness, and self-control in the lives of your children.

But my ultimate goal is not to provide a few gold nuggets

you can hand to your kids like Halloween candy. It's for you to become a miner and who will make miners out of your children. To teach them how to search for wisdom's treasures. Wisdom does not come gift-wrapped, lying at the foot of your bed each day. Like silver, it must be excavated from the mineshaft of God's Word.

God Loves Prospectors

Every time a miner discovers silver or gold, or someone discovers hidden treasure, it didn't just happen. Two things must be true for any miner or treasure hunter to strike gold. *First*, he must be *looking for it.* In the same way, we are told concerning wisdom, "look for it as for silver."[7] The Hebrew word translated "look" conveys the idea of a person relentlessly searching for something, believing that it exists and expecting to find it.[8] Just walking into a mine and glancing around won't produce anything. Ask any miner and he will tell you that gold doesn't strike you—you strike gold! But you will never strike gold unless you first go searching for it. Jewels of wisdom and understanding are "not usually discovered by a casual observer or a chance passerby. They are excavated and enjoyed instead by the diligent, devoted, and determined."[9]

> You must be determined every day to
> get into the Word of God so that
> the Word of God can get into you.

There's an old saying that "the devil is not afraid of a Bible that has dust on it." An unopened Bible is like a neglected gold mine—it may be rich with gold, but people never mind that it is never mined. It is sad to know that while 93 percent of Americans own a Bible, half never read it, including 23 percent of all born-again

Christians. According to Barna Research Group, only 18 percent of Christians read the Bible every day.[10]

The analogy is simple: If you want to mine for God's wisdom, you must be determined every day to get into the Word of God so that the Word of God can get into you.

Dad, I beg you to engage in regular Bible study and to encourage your children to do the same. Don't lean on that dusty excuse, "The reason why I don't read it is because I don't understand it." Invest in a readable contemporary translation, such as the New International Version or the New Living Translation, and read it every day. And don't claim to be too busy. We all have time to do what we really want to do. I share the sentiments of former President Woodrow Wilson:

> I am sorry for men who do not read the Bible every day; I wonder why they deprive themselves of the strength and of the pleasure. It is one of the most singular books in the world, for every time you open it, some old text that you have read a score of times suddenly beams with a new meaning. There is no other book that I know of, of which this is true; there is no other book that yields its meaning so personally, that seems to fit itself so intimately to the very spirit that is seeking its guidance.

The *second characteristic* of a miner is that not only must he be looking for gold, he also must be *digging for it.* You have access to two tools to help you dig for gold from the Bible.

First, *the Holy Spirit* can reveal the truth about what you're reading. The same Holy Spirit who revealed the wisdom of God's Word to the apostles and early Christians is also with you.

Years ago I heard about a man who loved to study the Bible. Every time he came to something he did not understand, his friend, Charlie, would pop into his mind. Charlie was a great

Bible student; he just seemed to ooze with biblical wisdom. Whenever this man encountered a Bible question, he would go to Charlie and say, "Charlie, what does this verse mean? What is God trying to say here?" One day, as this man was reading his Bible, the Holy Spirit of God spoke to him and said, "Why don't you ask Me? I'm the one who teaches Charlie."

Every Christian has within him the Spirit of revelation. The Holy Spirit yearns to speak to you through the Word of God. A great prayer to say as you begin your mining is, "Open my eyes that I may see wonderful things in your law."[11]

Second, you have *prayer* as a tool. Bible study and prayer must go together. You should pray before you read the Bible that God will help you to understand it, and then you should pray after you read the Bible that God will help you to apply what He has told you. God is like a faraway lover. The Bible is His letter communicating to you; prayer is the telephone you pick up to talk to Him.

> You have not completed the training of your children until you have modeled for them a strong walk with God.

Dad, it's crucial that you maintain a consistent daily time of Bible study and prayer with God. You have not completed the training of your children until you have modeled for them a strong walk with God. That's the best way to motivate them toward the same.

Bill Nelson, a former congressman from Florida, flew on a space shuttle mission aboard the *Columbia* just prior to the *Challenger* disaster. He wrote a book titled *Mission* describing his experience and explaining, among other things, how difficult it is to maintain a proper orbit in space.

There is no resistance in space, so an astronaut can literally turn that huge orbiter over by himself. To maintain a proper orbit, the onboard computers constantly make course and altitude corrections by firing small rockets that make minute adjustments. Larger jets burn to make major adjustments. These rockets are critical, for if they don't consistently fire at the right time, the space vehicle can veer from its orbit and either go tumbling into outer space or crashing into earth's atmosphere.[12]

In a similar way, left to ourselves we will tend to veer out of orbit into lukewarmness and indifference or into sin and downright rebellion. The twin rockets of prayer and Bible study "fired" continually and consistently will help us stay on course and prevent our lives from spinning out of spiritual control.

I want to give you seven questions that you can pass along to your children to take to the Scriptures every time you read them. When you use these questions, what you thought was hard rock will begin to yield the gold and silver of wisdom in abundance.

1. Is there a warning to heed?

2. Is there a promise to claim?

3. Is there a sin to forsake?

4. Is there a command to obey?

5. Is there a lesson to learn?

6. Is there a principle to apply?

7. Is there an example to follow?

As you ask yourselves those questions, keep a journal and write down the answers you mine—and what God gives you, pass along to your children.

Your kids can also be trained to have their own time with God using these same techniques. My children will tell you that when they were young, I encouraged them to spend time each morning in the Word and in prayer. They even took up my habit of reading Proverbs daily.

It's Not Too Early

Make sure that you lead your children to Christ personally and as early as you feel comfortable. You must be careful to make sure they understand the basic truths you're imparting to them, but do not doubt that they can come to a genuine faith decision at an early age if raised in a proper, spiritual atmosphere.

Some of the greatest Christians who ever lived made decisions to follow Jesus when they were young: Jonathan Edwards (age eight), Charles Spurgeon (age twelve), Bible commentator Matthew Henry (age eleven), and the courageous early church martyr Polycarp (age nine).

You may not be a pastor, *but you are the spiritual leader in your home.* Here are some suggestions to guide you as you take the lead in leading your children to Christ.

- Begin when they are young and read Bible stories to them. Let them hear you pray for them to know Jesus personally, constantly thanking Jesus for loving us enough to die for our sins.

- As you take them to church, explain what the various rituals and seasons (baptism, the Lord's Supper, Easter, Christmas) represent and why they are observed and celebrated.

- Be sensitive to every spiritual question they ask and take the time to answer their questions thoroughly and in a way they can understand.

- Trust the Holy Spirit to give you wisdom at the right time to clearly present the gospel to them, and pray continuously for their salvation.

A woman came to her pastor and said, "Pastor, how early should I start the serious spiritual training of my child?"

"How old is the child?" the pastor asked.

"Five."

"Lady," the pastor said, "you are five years too late."

Timing is everything, and the earlier you train your child the better. Be cautious if your child makes an early faith decision but do not discourage it.

On one occasion preacher Dwight L. Moody reported "two and one-half conversions" at a service he conducted. One person said, "I suppose you mean two adults and one child."

"No," Moody replied. "I mean two children and one adult. The children can give their whole lives to God, but the adult has only half of his left to give."

The Father Your Child Can Have

Some time ago, someone wrote a little piece titled "What America Needs." I thought the anonymous author put it perfectly. America needs:

- a leader like Moses who was determined to obey God no matter what

- army generals like Joshua who knew God and could pray and shout things to pass rather than blow them to pieces with atomic energy

- politicians like Joseph who walked with God and sought His will for all policies

- preachers like Peter who had the courage to look people in the eye and say, "Repent or perish" and denounce personal as well as national sins

- mothers like Hannah who would pray for their children and give them to God, rather than become delinquent mothers of delinquent children

- children like Samuel who would talk to God in the hours of the night and honor their parents in the hours of the day

- physicians like Luke who would not only care for physical needs and treat human life both in and out of the womb as something sacred, but would also introduce their patients to the Great Physician, the Lord Jesus Christ

- a God like Israel's, not the man upstairs but a thrice Holy God who blesses holiness and curses sinfulness

- a Savior like Jesus who can save anyone at any time, at any place, including an entire world, if they would just turn to Him

America needs strong, committed, godly dads with the integrity, convictions, and dedication to teach their kids that in a world often headed the wrong way, God's way is the right way.

I would add to this list that America needs strong, committed, godly dads with the integrity, convictions, and dedication to teach their kids that in a world often headed the wrong way, God's way is the right way.

Your children must not only hear wisdom taught; they must see wisdom lived. That is why your time with God every day is so important. It is that time spent alone with the Lord that not only gives you wisdom but also strengthens your heart. The devotional life consistently practiced is critically important. So, be a dad who models the fear of God in his own life.

In 1993, workers made a remarkable discovery while doing some renovations at the Baseball Hall of Fame in Cooperstown,

New York. Tucked away under a display case was an old photograph of a baseball player who was never formally inducted into the famous museum. The man had a bat on his shoulder and wore a uniform with "Sinclair Oil" printed across the chest. Stapled to the picture was a handwritten note: "You were never too tired to play ball. On your days off, you helped build the Little League field. You always came to watch me play. You were a Hall of Fame Dad. I wish I could share this moment with you. Your son, Peter."

C. Everett Koop, former surgeon general of the United States, has soberly observed: "Life affords no greater responsibility, no greater privilege than the raising of the next generation."[13] When our homes become factories of divine wisdom manufacturing wise children, this nation can be turned around—and the head of that factory is to be you, dad.

At the risk of beating the drum one time too many, the greatest thing you will ever give your children is wisdom from God, for the reward of wisdom is, as Solomon said, "Then you will understand the fear of the LORD and find the knowledge of God."[14] You cannot give your children two greater rewards than the fear of the Lord and the knowledge of God. They must fear the Lord before they can know Him, but they must also know Him before they are prepared to live for Him in the present and meet Him in the future.

Solomon knew long ago what we should know now—that divine wisdom, imparted parentally, consistently, and practically, will turn your child into a champion for God. That remains my prayer for you and your children.

Is There a Hero in the House?

"The child is the father of the man."
WILLIAM WORDSWORTH

When I was a child, I always wanted to be Superman. I even had a blue-and-red costume with the iconic "S" on the front that made me feel as if I could bend metal bars and see through walls. My mother often worried that my fascination for the Man of Steel would end up hurting me, that I'd jump off a rooftop or step in front of a car. She was almost right on more than one occasion, but she never squashed my childhood imagination. She knew that every child needs a hero.

Today, as I look out at a world filled with violence, consumerism, and sexuality, I have to ask, *Where are the heroes? Where are the men and women we can't help but look up to? Where are those we may confidently pattern our lives after?*

A man entered a barbershop and noticed a teenage boy sweeping the floor. The man struck up a conversation with the fellow and soon learned that the boy had no father in his life.

"Son," the man asked, "who do you want to be like when you grow up?"

"Mister, I ain't never met nobody that I want to be like when I grow up."

That story mirrors the situation an increasing number of children face. Author Warren Wiersbe observed:

> We live in a world in which real heroes are scarce and we have to settle for substitutes, such as overrated movie stars and overpaid athletes and rock singers, people who are famous only for being famous and, of course, for being rich. Even some of our favorite heroes of history have been reclassified by revisionist historians so that their achievements don't shine as gloriously as they once did. So, whether you're reading a history textbook, a new biography, or *Time*, you're probably finding it more and more difficult to discover somebody worthy of admiration, somebody you can call a hero or a heroine.[1]

He's right and leaves us with a lingering question about who will light the way forward for twenty-first-century children. The villain in the newest *Iron Man* movie proclaims, "Heroes? There is no such thing." But this is a great lie, and I wonder if truth is found not in comic books but in our homes. Could the hero be you?

> Having raised three children into adulthood, I now believe that at least one of every child's heroes should be their dad.

Having raised three children into adulthood, I now believe that at least one of every child's heroes should be their dad. Looking back over my sons' lives, I now recognize I wasn't always the hero I should have been. I was often too busy, too unplugged, too disconnected to be their Superman. This realization forms one of the greatest regrets of my life.

Searching for Superman

Two things must happen for you to become your children's hero. First, *you must be willing*. A father must want to lead. If your children sense that your desire to lead is not present, their desire to follow will be absent. Even with all of your other responsibilities at work, church, and in the community, you must demonstrate a "fire in the belly" to be proactive in leading your kids. You must be willing to pay the price if you are going to be the father of your family—and you will pay a higher price if you are not.

Second, *you must be present*. A dad must be available and accessible. Period. I wasn't always present when my children were young and I should've been. I hope you'll learn this now and avoid similar mistakes.

Do you want to be a good father? Then memorize and live by this acrostic:

Direction
Availability
Discipline
Spirituality

The one crucial component in the above list is *availability*. If you are not available, you cannot give direction, your discipline will be resented, and your spiritual leadership will be rejected. Let me substitute one word in the above acrostic and watch what happens:

Direction
Unavailability
Discipline
Spirituality

The difference between a *dad* and a *dud* is simple. It's the difference between availability and unavailability. You can father a child, but unless you are available you will not live up to the title.

I can't think of anything more tragic than to have your children not even notice when you are gone. When I would be out of town for an extended time, one of the first things I would ask Teresa is, "Did the boys miss me?" I was always relieved when she told me they did.

Dad, do your children notice when you're gone? If you're not missed, you're missing it.

Nature abhors a vacuum. If you don't lead your children, someone else will lead them for you. If you're not there for your children, someone else will be there for them. If you refuse to be the hero in their life, they will find another hero, and it may be someone you don't like. When that happens, the greater problem is not that you won't be around, but that you will no longer be missed!

Years ago I went with my youngest son, Joshua, to the Six Flags Over Georgia theme park along with his fourth-grade class. I dutifully tagged along as he rode several rides with one of his classmates, who was there with his mother. The mom and I struck up a conversation, and I discovered that she and her son had recently joined our church. When I asked if her husband was also a member, she said the only time he had attended our church was when she and her son had been baptized. She then began to open her soul and bare the heartache caused by her workaholic, absentee father-husband. "He is a good man, but he doesn't even see the need to accompany our son on things like this. I run my own business, and he could not understand why I would miss a day of making money just to waste a day at Six Flags with my son."

Her next statement crushed me, both for the son and the father. "Pastor, my son is so accustomed now to the fact that his dad does not spend time with him, he didn't even bother to ask him to come."

My son's class left the park early, but I stayed until the park closed to spend another three hours alone with my boy. I will never forget as we were walking out of the park—covered in white sugar, the remnants of a shared funnel cake—Joshua stopped me, gave me a big hug, and said, "Dad, thanks for taking me to Six Flags. You are my very best friend." Hearing that was something that could not be bought on eBay. It still brings tears to my eyes today. If you want to lead your children, be willing and be present.

We live in an age when kids have more of the things they want and less of the things they need. Our kids wear name-brand clothes, fill their pockets with money we give them, and drive their own cars while listening to iPods on state-of-the-art sound systems. I wonder which is true: Do they not have a dad? Or do they have an absentee dad who doesn't care?

> I think most dads today would say they love their children. But we must all remind ourselves that love is not spelled t-h-i-n-g-s; it is spelled t-i-m-e.

I think most dads today would say they love their children. But we must all remind ourselves that love is not spelled t-h-i-n-g-s; it is spelled t-i-m-e. Your kids need *you* more than they need the trinkets, treasures, and toys you can buy them (and that is also true for your wife).

Where are you, dad? Are you loving by giving your children things or time? Are you more likely to be found in an airport or at a soccer game? Don't be like so many fathers who can be found almost anywhere except in the company of their children.

Do you genuinely want to be a hero to your children? I hope so. Every dad should desire to impact his kids' lives for goodness and godliness. If you are able to do this successfully, your influence on them will live for generations.

The great Bible teacher R.A. Torrey (1856–1928) made a statement that should shake all of us dads to our very core: "A man's success as a Christian leader cannot be determined until one sees his grandchildren." Dad, *you are raising not only sons and daughters, you are raising future fathers and mothers.*

Gordon MacDonald tells the following story:

> Among the legends is the tale of a medieval sidewalk superintendent who asked three stone masons on a construction project what they were doing. The first replied that he was laying bricks. The second described his work as that of building a wall. But it was the third laborer who demonstrated genuine esteem for his work when he said, "I am raising a great cathedral."
>
> Pose that same question to any two fathers concerning their role in the family, and you are liable to get the same kind of contrast. The first may say, "I am supporting a family." But the second may see things differently and say, "I am raising children." The former looks at his job as putting bread on the table. But the latter sees things in God's perspective: He is participating in the shaping of lives.[2]

As dads, this is exactly what we're doing—shaping lives today that tomorrow will be shaping the lives of future generations. So though our journey has come to its final stop, yours continues on. My challenge for you remains unchanged:

You are already a dad. Go become the kind of dad God wants you to be.

NOTES

Introduction: Being Fathers in a World of Fatherlessness

1. Maureen Downey, "Restoring Fatherhood Can Benefit U.S. Culture," *Atlanta Journal-Constitution,* 29 May 1995.

2. Cited in David Blankenhorn, *Fatherless America* (New York: Basic Books, 1995), 1. The study cited was published in 1984. However, since nonmarital child-bearing has increased dramatically since 1984, this estimation of "about half" is probably too low.

3. Don Feder, "Fatherless Families Fuel Crime Explosion," *Conservative Chronicle,* 21 November 1993. italics added.

4. Ibid.

5. Ralph Reed, *Politically Incorrect* (Dallas: Word, 1994), 87.

6. Cited by David Moore, *Five Lies of the Century* (Wheaton, IL: Tyndale House Publishers, 1995), 89.

7. *In Other Words,* May/June 1995.

8. Charles Colson, *A Dance with Deception* (Dallas: Word, 1993), 178.

9. Dick Williams, *The Atlanta Journal,* n.d.

10. William J. Bennett, *The Broken Hearth* (New York, NY: Doubleday, 2001), 92-93.

11. Stephen R. Covey, *The Seven Habits of Highly Effective People* (New York: Simon and Schuster, 1989), 95-104.

Chapter 1: God's Letter to Dads

1. 2 Chronicles 1:7.

2. David Jeremiah, *The Wisdom of God* (Milford, MI: Mott Media, n.d.), 73.

3. 2 Chronicles 1:10.

4. 2 Chronicles 1:11-12.

5. Patrick M. Morley, *The Seven Seasons of a Man's Life* (Nashville, TN: Thomas Nelson Publishers, 1995), 58.

6. Proverbs 8:11.

7. Proverbs 4:7.

8. Warren Wiersbe's thought here is important to note: "Remember that the Hebrew society was strongly masculine and that primarily the fathers trained the sons while the mothers trained the daughters. The masculine emphasis in Scripture must not be interpreted as a sexist bias, but

174   What God Wants Every Dad to Know

rather as a characteristic of the Jewish culture of that day, a characteristic that should no longer persist in the light of the gospel (Gal. 3:26-29)." Warren Wiersbe, *Be Skillful* (Wheaton, IL: Victor Books, 1995), 170.

9. Proverbs 1:8; 3:12; 4:1,3; 10:1; 15:20; 17:25; 19:13,26; 20:20; 23:22,24,25; 28:7,24; 29:3; 30:11,17.

10. Proverbs 4:1-4.

11. Proverbs 4:5-7.

12. Proverbs 4:10-11.

13. Haddon Robinson, from the foreword to Robert L. Alden, *Proverbs: A Commentary on an Ancient Book of Timeless Advice* (Grand Rapids, MI: Baker Books, 1983), 12.

14. Quoted in H. Wayne House and Kenneth M. Durham, *Living Wisely in a Foolish World: A Contemporary Look at the Wisdom of Proverbs* (Nashville, TN: Thomas Nelson Publishers, 1992), 12-13.

15. Quoted in Eleanor Doan, *A Speakers Sourcebook* (Grand Rapids, MI: Zondervan, 1960), 284.

16. Proverbs 2:6.

17. 1 Corinthians 1:25.

18. David C. Needham, *Close to His Majesty* (Portland, OR: Multnomah Press, 1987), 8.

19. James 1:5.

20. Steve Farrar, *Standing Tall* (Sisters, OR: Multnomah Publishers, 1994), 201.

21. Proverbs 1:20-21.

Chapter 2: Learn to Discern Between Friends, Foes, and Fools

1. Proverbs 18:24.

2. Proverbs 18:24 NKJV.

3. *Bits and Pieces*, 14 October 1993.

4. Proverbs 12:26.

5. Proverbs 18:24.

6. Charles Colson, *Life Sentence* (Lincoln, VA: Chosen Books, 1979), 79.

7. Proverbs 24:17-20.

8. Romans 12:19.

9. Allen P. Ross, "Proverbs," *The Expositor's Bible Commentary*, Frank E. Gaebelein, gen. ed. (Grand Rapids, MI: Zondervan, 1991), 1084.

10. Charles R. Swindoll, *Active Spirituality* (Dallas: Word Publishing, 1994), 129.

11. Proverbs 1:7.

12. Proverbs 10:21.

13. Proverbs 14:7.

14. Proverbs 12:26.

15. Proverbs 4:14-17.

16. Proverbs 13:20.

17. Proverbs 1:10-16.

18. Proverbs 10:1; 15:5.

19. Proverbs 10:32; 15:28.
20. Proverbs 29:22.
21. Proverbs 22:11.
22. Proverbs 18:24.
23. His son *was* being honest, by the way. The man who "walked on the trees" was a telephone repairman with equipment on his boots for climbing.

Chapter 3: It Doesn't Take Much to Say a Lot

1. R.F. Horton, *The Expositor's Bible*, vol. 4, *The Book of Proverbs* (New York: A.C. Armstrong and Son, 1898), 163-64.
2. Robert B. Downs, *Books that Change the World* (New York: New American Library, 1956), 129.
3. Proverbs 18:21.
4. Proverbs 23:15-16.
5. Proverbs 13:3.
6. Proverbs 11:13.
7. Proverbs 16:28.
8. R. Laird Harris, Gleason L. Archer Jr., and Bruce K. Waltke, *Theological Wordbook of the Old Testament* (Chicago: Moody Press, 1980), 2:848.
9. Proverbs 20:19.
10. 1 Timothy 5:19 NKJV.
11. Proverbs 10:19 NKJV.
12. Proverbs 29:20.
13. Proverbs 28:23.
14. Proverbs 27:21.
15. Proverbs 15:28.
16. Proverbs 10:32.
17. *USA Today*, 28 January 1988.
18. Proverbs 5:21.
19. Luke 12:2-3.
20. Proverbs 25:11-12.
21. Ronald Dunn, *The Faith Crisis* (Wheaton, IL: Tyndale House Publishers, 1984), 123-24.
22. Proverbs 17:27-28.
23. Proverbs 11:13.
24. Proverbs 17:9.
25. Proverbs 12:25.
26. Deuteronomy 6:5-7.

Chapter 4: Lower Your Temper-ature

1. Psalm 4:4 NKJV.

2. John 2:13-16.

3. Isaiah 5:20-23,25.

4. Bill Webber, *Conquering the Kill-Joys* (Waco, TX: Word Books, 1986), 30.

5. *Atlanta Journal-Constitution*, 11 May 1989.

6. *Illustrations for Biblical Preaching*, ed. Michael P. Green (Grand Rapids, MI: Baker Book House, 1989), 20.

7. Luke 23:34.

8. Proverbs 14:17.

9. Proverbs 15:18a.

10. Proverbs 19:19.

11. Proverbs 16:32 NKJV.

12. Proverbs 15:18.

13. Proverbs 14:29.

14. Proverbs 15:1.

15. Proverbs 19:11.

16. Proverbs 29:11.

Chapter 5: Develop the Discipline of Discipline

1. Hosea 8:7.

2. "Fortress-like Dallas School Points Way," *Atlanta Journal-Constitution*, 25 September 1995.

3. D. Bruce Lockerbie, *Who Educates Your Child?* (Garden City, NY: Doubleday, 1980), 92-93.

4. Proverbs 22:6 NKJV.

5. H. Wayne House and Kenneth M. Durham, *Living Wisely in a Foolish World* (Nashville: Thomas Nelson Publishers, 1992), 68.

6. Proverbs 19:18 NLT.

7. Proverbs 13:24 MSG.

8. Ibid.

9. *Golf Digest*, March 2005, 150.

10. Zig Ziglar, *Raising Positive Kids in a Negative World* (Nashville: Oliver Nelson, 1985), 216.

11. Proverbs 3:11-12.

12. Proverbs 22:15 NLT.

13. Proverbs 29:15 NLT.

14. Proverbs 29:17.

15. Proverbs 23:13-14 NLT.

16. Proverbs 10:13; 13:24; 22:15; 23:13-14; 26:3; 29:15.

17. Walter C. Kaiser Jr., *Hard Sayings of the Old Testament* (Downers Grove, IL: InterVarsity Press, 1988), 180-81.

18. Derek Kidner, *The Proverbs: An Introduction and Commentary* (Downers Grove, IL: InterVarsity Press, 1964), 147.

19. J. Oswald Sanders, *A Spiritual Clinic* (Chicago: Moody Press, 1958), 90.

20. Kaiser wisely reminds us, "As with many other moral proverbs of this sort, the question often comes from many a distraught parent: 'Does this proverb have any exceptions to it, or will it always work out that if we train our children as this verse advises us, we can be sure they won't turn from the Lord?'

"No, this verse is no more an ironclad guarantee than is any other proverb in this same literary category. As in many other universal and definite moral prescriptions (Proverbs) it tells us only what generally takes place without implying there are no exceptions to the rule. The statement is called a proverb, not a promise. Many godly parents have raised their children in ways that were genuinely considerate of the children's own individuality and the high calling of God, yet the children have become rebellious and wicked despite their parents' attempts to bring about different results." Kaiser, *Hard Sayings*, 181.

21. Proverbs 13:1.

Chapter 6: Don't Be Afraid of Birds or Bees

1. Alice Park, "Parents' Sex Talk with Kids: Too Little, Too Late," *Time,* 7 December 2009, www.time.com/time/health/article/0,8599,1945759,00.html.

2. Ibid.

3. Proverbs 5:23.

4. Cited in Stuart Briscoe, *Choices of a Lifetime* (Wheaton, IL: Tyndale House Publishers, 1995), 95.

5. Allen Ginsberg, Sandra L. Hanson, and David E. Myers, "Responsibility and Knowledge: Their Role in Reducing Out-of-Wedlock Childbearing" (Washington, DC: Department of Education).

6. Proverbs 7:6-8.

7. Elisabeth Elliot, *Passion and Purity* (Old Tappan, NJ: Fleming H. Revell, 1983), 147.

8. Proverbs 7:13-18.

9. Proverbs 2:16 NKJV.

10. Proverbs 5:3.

11. Proverbs 6:23-24.

12. Proverbs 7:5.

13. Proverbs 7:21.

14. Proverbs 7:21-23 MSG.

15. Proverbs 5:3-5 MSG.

16. Proverbs 6:27-29 MSG.

17. Cal Thomas, *The Things that Matter Most* (New York: Harper College Publishers, 1994), 82.

18. "Abstinence: The Radical Choice for Sex-Ed," *Christianity Today,* February 1993, 27.

19. Glenn P. Dewberry Jr., "Reducing the Risk of AIDS in High School Students: Lifelong Monogamy Is the Moral Solution," *Journal of the American Medical Association,* 19 January 1994.

20. Proverbs 5:14 NLT.

21. Charles Swindoll, *The Finishing Touch* (Dallas: Word Publishing, 1994), 105.

22. Proverbs 5:15-19.

Chapter 7: Work Is Important...But It's Not Everything

1. Genesis 2:2.

2. Genesis 2:15.

3. Mark 6:3.

4. Acts 18:1-3.

5. Proverbs 26:14.

6. Derek Kidner, *The Proverbs: An Introduction and Commentary* (Downers Grove, IL: InterVarsity Press, 1964), 42.

7. Proverbs 19:15.

8. Proverbs 20:13.

9. Proverbs 6:9.

10. Proverbs 10:5.

11. Proverbs 19:15.

12. 2 Thessalonians 3:10.

13. Proverbs 12:27 NKJV.

14. Proverbs 19:24.

15. Proverbs 6:9.

16. Proverbs 21:25.

17. Robert Hicks, *In Search of Wisdom* (Colorado Springs, CO: NavPress, 1995), 50.

18. Proverbs 26:16.

19. Proverbs 15:19.

20. Proverbs 22:13; see also 26:13.

21. Proverbs 20:4.

22. Quoted in A.L. Williams, *All You Can Do Is All You Can Do, and All You Can Do Is Enough* (Nashville: Oliver Nelson, 1988), 61.

23. Proverbs 18:9.

24. Charles R. Swindoll, *Active Spirituality* (Dallas: Word Publishing, 1994), 106.

25. Proverbs 10:26.

26. Proverbs 24:33-34.

27. Proverbs 6:6-8.

28. Bill Gothard, *Men's Manual,* vol. 2 (Oak Brook, IL: Institute in Basic Youth Conflicts, 1983), 226.

29. *Merriam-Webster's Eleventh Collegiate Dictionary.*

30. Proverbs 16:26.

31. Proverbs 14:23 NKJV.

32. R.C. Sproul, *Pleasing God* (Wheaton, IL: Tyndale House Publishers, 1988), 179.

33. *Atlanta Journal-Constitution,* 2 September 1996.

34. Gothard, *Men's Manual,* 229.

35. Ibid.

36. Larry Burkett, "Retirement Goals," *Moody Monthly,* February 1995, 34.

37. John 17:4.

38. http://stats.oecd.org/Index.aspx?DatasetCode=ANHRS.

39. Pat Williams, *Go for the Magic* (Nashville: Thomas Nelson Publishers, 1995), 137.

Chapter 8: Strive to Be Fiscally Fit

1. Patrick Morley, *The Man in the Mirror* (Brentwood, TN: Wolgemuth and Hyatt Publishers, 1989), 130.

2. Norman Cousins, *Human Options* (New York: W.W. Norton, 1981), 103.

3. Morley, *Man in the Mirror,* 110.

4. "American Household Credit Card Debt Statistics through 2012," www.nerdwallet.com/blog/credit-card-data/average-credit-card-debt-household/.

5. Deuteronomy 8:18.

6. Proverbs 10:4.

7. Proverbs 12:11; see also Proverbs 28:19.

8. Proverbs 13:11.

9. Proverbs 22:16.

10. Proverbs 28:8.

11. See Matthew 6:24.

12. Proverbs 13:8 NLT.

13. Morley, *Man in the Mirror,* 131.

14. Proverbs 1:19.

15. Robert C. Larson, *The Best of Ted Engstrom* (San Bernardino, CA: Here's Life Publishers, 1988), 17.

16. Larry Burkett, *Answers to Your Family's Financial Questions* (Pomona, CA: Focus on the Family Publishing, 1987), 52.

17. Proverbs 15:27.

18. Quoted in James C. Dobson, *Love for a Lifetime* (Portland, OR: Multnomah Press, 1987), 70-71.

19. Proverbs 30:7-9.

20. "Who's Happy?" *Christianity Today,* 23 November 1992, 24.

21. Proverbs 23:4-5.

22. Proverbs 3:9-10.

23. Rick Bragg, "A Thief Dines Out, Hoping Later to Eat In," *New York Times,* 19 May 1994, www.nytimes.com/1994/05/19/nyregion/a-thief-dines-out-hoping-later-to-eat-in.html.

24. Wayne House and Kenneth M. Durham, *Living Wisely in a Foolish World* (Nashville: Thomas Nelson Publishers, 1992), 41-42.

25. Proverbs 22:7.

26. Psalm 37:21.

27. see Proverbs 6:1-5; 11:15; 17:18; 22:26-27.

28. Proverbs 6:8.

29. Proverbs 13:7.

30. Proverbs 28:6.

31. Proverbs 15:16.

32. Albert M. Wells Jr., *Inspiring Quotations* (Nashville: Thomas Nelson Publishers, 1988), 129.

Chapter 9: Be Good and Be Godly

1. Ecclesiastes 12:12.

2. Ecclesiastes 12:13.

3. Ecclesiastes 12:13b.

4. Ecclesiastes 12:14.

5. William Kilpatrick, *Why Johnny Can't Tell Right from Wrong* (New York: Simon and Schuster, 1992), 248-49.

6. Proverbs 2:4.

7. Proverbs 2:4a.

8. R. Laird Harris, Gleason L. Archer Jr., and Bruce K. Waltke, *Theological Wordbook of the Old Testament* (Chicago: Moody Press, 1980), 1:126.

9. Robert L. Alden, *Proverbs: A Commentary on an Ancient Book of Timeless Advice* (Grand Rapids, MI: Baker Book House, 1983), 32.

10. "Survey Shows Lack of Bible Reading," *Moody Monthly,* February 1989.

11. Psalm 119:18.

12. Bill Nelson with Jamie Buckingham, *Mission: An American Congressman's Voyage to Space* (New York: Harcourt, Brace, Jovanovich, 1988), 120.

13. *In Other Words,* Winter 1996, 3.

14. Proverbs 2:5.

Conclusion: Is There a Hero in the House?

1. Warren Wiersbe, *Preaching and Teaching with Imagination* (Wheaton, IL: Victor Books, 1994), 237.

2. Gordon MacDonald, *The Effective Father* (Wheaton, IL: Tyndale House Publishers, 1977), 183-84.

ACKNOWLEDGMENTS

Working on a book must be something like birthing a baby—there is no pain like it, but the product is worth it, at least to the ones who endured the process. I have learned that though a book has only one author, it has many contributors. I want to thank all who made invaluable contributions to this book.

To the team at Harvest House, a big shout out! You are such a joy to work with, and I am grateful for you all.

To my editor, Rod Morris, thanks for making me look good and for your patience.

To Eric and Robert Wolgemuth, thanks for continuing to work with me and advocate on my behalf. You are more than agents; you are my friends.

To a great church family at Cross Pointe, who gives me space and time to work on projects such as these. Your supernatural hunger for God's Word and God's work inspires me!

To my three wonderful sons, James Jr., Jonathan, and Joshua, you are the greatest! I love you more than life itself. With you guys there is never a dull moment, but I wouldn't have it any other way. A special thank you to my middle son, Jonathan, whose editorial insights and revisions pushed this project over the finish line.

To my daughter-in-law Natalie, thanks for being a great mom to Harper and Presley. I'm so glad James married you!

To my grandchildren, Harper and Presley, Pop adores you and will give you anything you want!

To my very best friend and soul mate, my darling wife, Teresa. I still can't figure out why you married me—but thank God you did. If you ever leave me, I'm going with you! Solomon was right when he said, "a prudent wife is from the LORD" (Proverbs 19:14). You certainly are.

May my Father in heaven be glorified in this effort and use it to mature men into fathers who are more like Him.

ABOUT THE AUTHOR

James Merritt is senior pastor of Cross Pointe Church in Duluth, Georgia, and the host of *Touching Lives*, a television show that broadcasts weekly in all 50 states and 122 countries. He formerly served as a two-term president of the Southern Baptist Convention, America's largest Protestant denomination. He is the author of eight books including *Still Standing: 8 Winning Strategies for Facing Tough Times* and *How to Impact and Influence Others: 9 Keys to Successful Leadership* (both with Harvest House).

As a national voice on faith and leadership, he has been interviewed by *Time*, *Fox News*, *ABC World News*, *MSNBC*, and *60 Minutes*. Dr. Merritt holds a bachelor's degree from Stetson University and a master's and doctor of philosophy from Southern Baptist Theological Seminary. He and his wife, Teresa, reside outside of Atlanta near their three children and two grandchildren.

Follow him on twitter at @DrJamesMerritt.

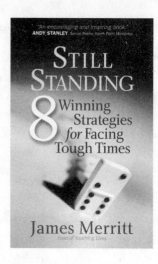

Still Standing
8 Winning Strategies for Facing Tough Times

Everybody faces tough times. No one gets a free pass from those make-or-break moments that lead to character development, achievement, and fulfillment.

The Bible is replete with stories of people who faced tough times and stood firm in their faith. From these stories, James Merritt uncovers guiding principles and winning strategies to help us face our own challenges and find victory in the midst of adversity. Examples include:

- Joseph, who illustrates how to respond when we get what we don't deserve

- Daniel, who inspires us to stand for what's right when no one else does or will

- Esther, who emboldens us to place the well-being of others above our own comfort and security

When life threatens to trip us up, push us over, or knock us down, we *can* stand tall. *Still Standing* points the way toward a life of freedom, joy, and victory as we discover God's winning strategies for tackling tough times head-on.

How to Impact and Influence Others
9 Keys to Successful Leadership

A person's character—who he is—determines the impact he has on others. James Merritt, senior pastor of Cross Pointe Church and host of the television program *Touching Lives*, unlocks nine key character qualities that, if consistently exercised and seen by others, will influence them to reach their full potential.

Readers of this book will be motivated to leave a lasting impact in a number of ways, such as

- making sure someone sees, hears, or feels love from them each day
- letting God's joy shine through their life
- being kind to someone every day
- being faithful and dependable
- treating others as more important

No one can do anything about his heritage, but he can do something about his legacy. Beginning today, he can become the kind of person who makes a life-changing difference for others, perhaps even an *eternal* difference. *How to Impact and Influence Others* shows the way to a life of surpassing influence.

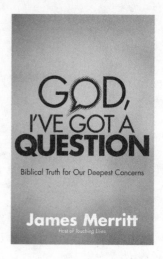

God, I've Got a Question
Biblical Truth for Our Deepest Concerns

James Merritt, popular pastor, author, and host of the television show *Touching Lives*, knows that when people wrestle with doubts, they are missing out on the security, promises, and power of Christ.

Avoiding academic lingo, Merritt presents relatable, relevant responses to the hard questions that seekers and Christians hesitate to ask or answer:

- Why is there so much suffering in the world if God is in control?

- How can I discover God's will for my life?

- Why is Jesus the only way to God, and how can I defend this?

- What should I do about the moral gray areas of my life?

- Why should anybody believe the Bible?

Whether read straight through or used as a reference for specific topics, this insightful resource reveals the uncompromised truths of the Christian faith and the depth and importance of its precepts for every person, every life.

To learn more about Harvest House books and
to read sample chapters, log on to our website:

www.harvesthousepublishers.com

HARVEST HOUSE PUBLISHERS
EUGENE, OREGON